MOM & KID

OTHER MARKETING BOOKS FROM PMP

The Kids Market: Myths & Realities

Marketing to American Latinos, Part I

Marketing to American Latinos, Part II

The Whole Enchilada

Beyond Bogedas: Developing a Retail Relationship
with Hispanic Customers

The Mirrored Window: Focus Groups
from a Moderator's Point of View

The Great Tween Buying Machine

Marketing Insights to Help Your Business Grow

Why People Buy Things They Don't Need

A Knight's Code of Business: How to Achieve
Character and Competence in the Corporate World

India Business: Finding Opportunities
in this Big Emerging Market

Moderating to the Max! A Full-tilt Guide to Creative
Focus Groups and Insightful Depth Interviews

Marketing to Leading-Edge Baby Boomers

Clear Eye for Branding: Straight Talk on
Today's Most Powerful Business Concept

Advertising to Baby Boomers

What's Black About It?: Insights to Increase Your
Share of a Changing African-American Market

Marketing to the
New Super Consumer
Mom & Kid

TIM COFFEY, DAVID SIEGEL

AND

GREG LIVINGSTON

PARAMOUNT MARKET PUBLISHING, INC.

Paramount Market Publishing, Inc.
301 S. Geneva Street, Suite 109
Ithaca, NY 14850
www.paramountbooks.com
Telephone: 607-275-8100; 888-787-8100   Facsimile: 607-275-8101

Publisher: James Madden
Editorial Director: Doris Walsh

Cataloging in Publication Data available
ISBN 0-9766973-2-7

Book design and composition: Paperwork

Contents

Preface

IT HAS LONG BEEN SAID that the way to a man's heart is through his stomach. Now we're here to say that the best way to a mom's heart is through—*her children.* Whether she has an infant, kid, tween, or teen, a mom today wants to be the best mom she can possibly be for that child and that means that an awful lot of what she does, what she buys, and what she demands of her family is centered around her children.

Help a mom teach her child, nourish her child, nurture her child, and most of all be the best darn mother she can be to her child, and you'll be her hero.

Through the years, we have been involved heavily with helping many of the country's leading consumer goods and services companies understand today's kids, how to market to them, and why they deserve to be marketed to. Over the past twenty-five or so years we were total believers and preachers that understanding today's kids and marketing to them in effective, fun ways both enhanced their lives and helped companies grow too. Well, we still believe this with all of our hearts—and more importantly with all of the business successes enjoyed by many marketers of kid products.

BUT. . . . Over the past few years we have also seen that marketing to kids for kids sake is just a small part of the total story.

This book will introduce you to a new more powerful concept, a concept of a new consumer. The child is *such an important part* of mom's life that, due to some very interesting circumstances that we will bring to your attention, she and her child have virtually joined together to affect the purchases of many of today's goods and services.

I was raised that adults make decisions and children comply without question or discussion. I disagree, and raise my children completely different. Children need opportunities to make decisions in youth in order to be able to make good decisions as adults. My children decide on a great deal in their lives, and I value their good sense in helping me make household decisions as well.

MOM OF GIRL AGED 2 TO 4
WonderGroup Kid Influence Study

The above quote epitomizes what we have learned about today's moms and how they are dramatically different from their predecessors. It, and many other quotes throughout this book come from a new 2005 *Mom/Kid Influence Study* we just completed among 800 moms of children aged 2 to 14. We have taken this study and put it together with our many years of research and consulting and advertising for many of today's leading companies in fields like food, beverages, toys, travel, entertainment, retailing, health and beauty, home décor and even household cleansing, in order to bring you this book.

Our goal is to try to awaken you to the simple truth that mom and children have become partners in consumerism. Moms want the best for their children and that includes teaching them to realize that they have the power to make their own choices and decisions—and these decisions count!

Part I of this book will further introduce you to this new consumer phenomenon, how and why it has happened, its economic impact, and how it thinks. Part II will provide some options that should help you to further research this market and develop your own specific media plans, creative, consumer promotions, and products to best suit this market.

Happy reading and thank you!

—T.C., D.S. & G.L.
AUGUST 2005

1

Introducing the New Super Consumer . . . Mom & Her Kid

(a k a 4i4I™ : The Four-Eyed, Four-Legged Consumer)

"HEY! YOU TALKIN' TO ME?" There are two times you do *not* want to hear this. The first (for me), is when you are walking alone at night on some dark, lonely street. The second, more relevant to our discussion, is when a consumer asks this question because she has no idea whether your product, promotion, or message is directed to her.

We all know that good marketing starts with a deep understanding of your consumer. How you define that consumer can mean the world when it comes to developing specific products, promotions, and advertising. Is your target a Mom? Dad? Child? Teen? Boy? Girl? How do they act, think, respond? Your consumer is not, as some practitioners wrongly assume a *household with kids*. Households are things; things don't buy.

Defining your consumer is particularly tough when dealing with the various products or services in which a mom and child are involved. Is it the mom or the child that is your target consumer? As you can guess from the title of this book, it is, many times, neither. Rather, it's a newly understood, very powerful hybrid that you will soon get to know in a very special way—a way that we think will open your eyes to an entirely new, more effective way in which to market.

The age-old practice for marketing most goods and services designed for family consumption has been to market these items directly to the housewife, or the mom of the family. After all, it is she who usually makes the final decision as to what to buy and it is almost always she who does the actual purchasing.

Even with the majority of mothers working, little has changed as far as her purchasing power. Moms manage 80 percent of household spending. They are still the primary homemaker and consider that very important, if not the most important role in their lives.

Importantly, being a "mom" plays such a major role in being a woman that it is a puzzle to us as to why so many marketers overlook this fact when trying to market to women in the first place. Many marketers interested in marketing to women, disregard the fact that 36 percent of all women aged 25 to 49 are *also* moms. In fact, more than half of all women in their 30s are moms to kids under the age of 12!

As one author for EPM's *Marketing to Women* so aptly puts it: "While the factors that motivate women's behavior as consumers are varied and layered, having children has such profound effects on women's lifestyles and attitudes that some marketers consider it the most crucial factor for change in women's shopping habits."

In fact, in an April 2005 presentation we gave at the Marketing to Women Conference in Chicago, we were the only ones to address the fact that women are moms too. So, when we brought this obviously simple fact to the attention of the attendees, and that this fact can be highly useful to any marketer who must market products or services to women, you could literally see the attendees' jaws drop.

If a company that wishes to market to women *does* remember that the woman it is trying to reach may also be a mom, it will see that there may be many more efficient and effective alternatives available for motivating that woman. If a product or service is in any way consumed by or in any way affects a younger member of the family, then the "mom" factor kicks in big time. And if you think about it, you'll see that there are many products and services that do this. Among them are banks, home improvements, vacations, automobiles, pharmaceuticals, health and beauty aids, educational services, medical services, and of course food and beverage.

Enough talking about moms for now, because as you'll quickly learn in this book, kids themselves have become an equally important part of the purchase decision equation. About the time of the late 1980s, a new marketing movement addressing the potential power of children in the role of family purchase decisions made its introduction. The 1987 book, *Children as Consumers: Insights and Implications,* by Dr. James U. McNeal opened the eyes of many marketers to look at children as a legitimate market. This book went a long way toward getting businesses to realize that the big power of children was not just in the limited purchasing that they did but rather *in the powerful influence they had over family purchases.* And, for the first time marketers began to realize the importance of marketing more goods and services directly *to* children.

After McNeal's book, many companies began to market directly to children, not just companies in the candy, toy and cereal industry, as before, but also firms in foods, beverages, travel, entertainment, health and beauty, technology, and even the family automobile! And equally as important, the media was now there to take advantage of this sizable audience. Network TV was joined by cable TV, MTV, and even more important, a plethora of new kid-targeted TV shows and kid-targeted magazines.

And since McNeal's book, marketing consultants and advertising agencies focused on marketing to children, including us, began teaching companies about the "Nag" factor of America's kids, or the "Pester Power" of Europe's children. Books like our own *Great Tween Buying Machine,* Acuff and Reiher's *What Kids Buy and Why* and McNeal's follow-up book *The Kids Market: Myths and Realities* along with numerous Marketing to Kids Conferences over the last fifteen years all continued to extol kids and their ability to nag. The old adage was: Market and advertise to the child and the child will nag or pester mom to buy!

But *now* there is yet again, something new! In the past few years, we have witnessed a dramatic change taking place in how children and moms deal with purchasing decisions. A miracle has happened. The "nagging, affected," child versus the "passive, victimized" mom is much less evident. The mom *versus* child is *old* school!

The Old School of Thought: Moms and kids are adversaries.

Rather, what we are now seeing is a new mom and child relationship. No longer is it mom *versus* child. Now it has become mom *and* her child. So strong is this consumer relationship—this partnership—that we see kid and mom as one, virtually joined at the hip, one "Four-Eyed, Four-Legged" consumer—a Super Consumer capable of affecting the purchase of more than $1 trillion in U.S. goods and services every year!

Four-Eyed, Four-Legged Consumer

Moms and kids are talking through everything from where to go for dinner, to what to buy for school, and even where to go on vacation. The 2004 Roper *Youth Report* "The Consensual Kid," suggests that moms (and dads) are now re-asserting themselves in areas that were the domain of kids, and kids are more likely than before to seek their parents consent or advice on many items.

Kids now actually seem to be on the same wavelength as their moms and dads.

The way in which an interacting parent and child behave is quite different than either of them would act alone. Dr. Langbourne Rust, a research consultant for children's marketers, presented an example of this in a 1994 speech to the SRI Marketing to Kids conference. In his example he explained that moms alone wouldn't buy kids' novelty products. Neither would kids, if they were alone, because kids by nature are conservative and generally go with what they think they know. But, because mom is present, she serves to reassure her child and defuse her child's apprehensions about a new, never-experienced product, thereby making the product more exciting and interesting to the child. Because the child is present, the mom feels a measure of joy, even excitement in seeing her child so pleased with an item. The result . . . A BUY!

Many marketers often ignore some key facts when it comes to today's moms.

First, moms feel their kids' feelings. They love it when their kids giggle, laugh, and generally otherwise get pleasure from a product. Anyone who has a child knows this. You feel things that you would not have allowed yourself to feel since you were a child yourself! As we often say: "Having a kid gives you license to be a kid again! It is one of the great experiences of life." One of our own managers who left us two years ago to become a full-time mom recently called us to say it all. Specifically:

> You know, I often really wondered why moms would buy some of the things they bought for their children and I always felt that I would never buy *my child* things like a Happy Meal. Now, I have to admit that even though Kyle is just 2 years old and has never asked for one, I couldn't help but buy him a Happy Meal just to see the expression on his face and the joy in his eyes.

Second, they are usually on the same side as their kids. Mom gets pleasure from giving things to her child that make her child happy.

In fact, she has a general *need* to please her children and affirm that she is a good mom. As one mom so aptly told us in a focus group:

> There is a day coming when I won't be buying stuff for my kids, so I like it because it makes them happy and that makes me feel good, and they think you have moved the world.

Third, they actually feel the strong need to teach their children, and teaching them to be consumers is one of their jobs. Mom encourages her children to take the risk of trying something new by reassuring them of the safety and taking the worry out of making certain decisions.

> I use grocery shopping with my child as a means of helping her make healthy choices for herself. Shopping for items other than food allows her to make choices regarding color combinations for clothes and choosing items based on needs versus wants. She is a pretty savvy little shopper at three.
>
> MOM OF GIRL AGE 3

To put some perspective on this new type of parent-child relationship, we must first realize that this is far from the first time we've seen changes in parenting styles.

Sabrina Neeley, Ph.D. and assistant professor of marketing at Miami University of Ohio points out that a "parent" is a product of the individual, the group, and the collective. A parent's own history and experiences define who she is as an individual and may influence how she chooses to raise her child. Experiences by other members of the group (i.e. another parent, family member, or close friend) are offered and may or may not be considered as the mother develops her own parenting "style." Additionally, she is also a product of the collective society, its norms and expectations of her and her child. Religious, political, or ethnic influences may intervene, as well as information provided by individuals, educational institutions, and the media in the larger culture.

Society appoints "experts" who are recognized as child development authorities and provide guidance and consultation to parents. In American middle-class families, the pediatrician often serves as a major source of cultural knowledge about development and behavior. In a late 1990's study of U.S. parents, pediatricians were cited as the most frequently used source of parenting information (42 percent of cases), followed by books (20 percent) often written by pediatricians. Friends (16 percent) and family (6 percent) comprised only a small proportion of the sources of influence and information (Harkness *et al.* 1996).

Early 20th Century Parenting

At the turn of the 20th century, the prevailing idea was that human behavior was predetermined by genetics and was generally, uncontrollable or unchangeable. John Watson, often known as the father of the "behaviorism" school of psychology, dramatically challenged this idea and advocated that human behavior was predictable and controllable. His experimental studies with a young child in the 1920s demonstrated that children could be conditioned or "taught" emotional response. These studies established that human behavior was malleable and could be changed. Watson promoted himself as an expert in child behavior and his ideas influenced parents for decades as they attempted to "mold" their children to meet certain ideals (Crain 1992; Watson 1924). Children's behavior was tightly controlled, often through punishments, in order to shape the child into a "proper" adult. While children were given the rights to behave as children, moms often ran a "tight ship" and children were not deemed to have the ability, or the need, to engage in independent decision making and behaviors until they were teenagers.

Mid-Century Parenting Ideas

In the 1930s, Dr. Benjamin Spock came onto the scene with new and radically different ideas about child rearing with his book, *Baby and*

Child Care. This pediatrician became the most well-known and widely trusted expert on child-rearing issues and his book became the most widely read book on child care ever written, according to Martin T. Stein, M.D. Dr. Spock's influence was widely felt for most of the 20th century as his books were published in multiple languages and updated for new generations of parents.

Dr. Spock broke from tradition by declaring that children actually seek independence at a much younger age. On the subject of disciplining children, Dr. Spock suggested that parents do not necessarily have to dominate their children in order to guide good behavior. He advocated that parents could be friendly, but firm, and consistent in their message, because the parent knows what is good for the child. He was the first to actually advise parents to give their children opportunities to make decisions and take initiative, but still provide firm leadership and require politeness and cooperation.

As the U.S. emerged from World War II and moved into the era of the baby boom, higher education and incomes, growing socio-economic status, and mass consumption, Dr. Spock warned parents about permissiveness and overindulgence of children. He acknowledged that it is easy for parents to overindulge their children out of guilt, desire that their children have what they themselves didn't, fear of what others might say, or even fear that their children will think they are not loved.

The 1970s

While Dr. Spock's ideas about child rearing were influential and reflected a shift in approach from the turn of the century, parenting ideas changed dramatically again as many of the Baby Boomer children of the 1940s and 1950s became parents of GenXers and were confronted with changing social ideas. Parenting philosophies of the 1970s and 1980s reflected the changes that were taking place in the larger society as baby boomers were coming out of the turbulent 1960s and into adulthood and parenthood. Many of the equal rights ideals of this generation were reflected in their advocacy of allowing children even more freedom of choice and a focus on the psychological nurturing of children. Additionally, the circle of "experts" in child development and behavior grew from pediatricians to include psychologists, teachers, and religious leaders.

In 1974, John Holt published the essay, *Escape from Childhood*, in which he advocated giving children the same rights as adults—the right to vote, work, own property, travel, choose a guardian, control one's learning, drive, use drugs, and have sex. While this perspective may be seen as quite radical, his underlying premise was that children should not be treated differently, or worse, than any adult in society.

A self-esteem movement began in the late 1970s and radically changed the way we saw adult-child interactions. The idea that children were capable of meeting life's challenges and were worthy of happiness, led to numerous parenting books that focused not on discipline and behavioral change, but on improving a child's self esteem. The belief was that children with high self-esteem would naturally engage in positive individual and social behaviors. These ideas also led to an overhaul of many school curriculums to include programs for building self-esteem. This philosophy was often equated with heaping constant and undeserved praise upon children and not allowing any child to experience failure or lack of participation in activities. While this approach held great promise for changing children's view of the world, themselves and others, it became a lightning rod and the excuse for what some considered "bad behavior" in the 1990s and the turn of the 21st century.

A Call for Discipline

In response to some of the more radical parenting ideas of the 1970s that advocated parents as "best friends" to their children and promoted less discipline of children, American parents saw a return to more traditional ideals of parenting.

Dr. James Dobson's religious perspectives on parenting greatly influenced a generation of parents beginning in the late 1970s through books such as *Dare to Discipline*. As Dobson stated in his 1978 book *The Strong-Willed Child*, "At the top of the list of 'dumb thinking' is the notion that children are somehow endangered by the conscientious leadership of their loving parents. . . . These [Parent Effectiveness Training] anti-authority views are directly contradictory to the teaching of Scripture. A child learns to yield to the authority of God by first learning to submit (rather than bargain) to the leadership of his parents."

Dobson's return to religious ideals of discipline and leadership has been highly influential in parenting approaches into the 21st century as he continues to publish books and inspire other religious leaders to write on the subject.

Similar sentiments were being communicated in parenting literature, though not tied to religious doctrine. "Children need the security of clearly enforced rules before they can begin to handle freedom" was the cry of a new generation of parenting experts (Kayne 1984). Writers such as Kayne advocated attention to a child's self-esteem, but with a balanced approach that also included clear rules of behavior, setting limits, and allowing natural consequences of decisions and behaviors.

The 1980s saw remarkable changes in the number of women earning college degrees and entering the workforce, as well as changes in family structures, and children being given more household responsibilities. At the same time, the influence and opportunities of child consumers became more evident as marketers turned their attention to kids and increased messages targeted directly to kids. Finally, the rapid growth of new communication technologies ushered in a dramatic change in access to international information and influences through global television and then the internet in the 1990s.

The 1990s and Early 2000s

As the century drew to a close and the new century emerged, parenting approaches seemed to be converging on a "middle of the road" approach that promotes firm, loving guidance rather than punishments; setting limits, but also allowing children the freedom to make independent decisions according to their developmental stage. GenX moms saw the mistakes that their parents made, and vowed to do it differently. Growth in information access and communication abilities meant that women were also widening their span of "expert" influence to include other mothers (i.e., *The Girlfriends' Guide*, and online chat forums) and even media personalities (*i.e.,* Oprah Winfrey, Dr. Phil).

Today's media is also extolling upon the need to be "smarter, better" parents seizing upon the idea that a generation of struggling adults were the result of "poor parenting." Recall that self-esteem became a buzzword more than 20 years ago, fueled by parenting experts, psychologists and educators. Believers suggested that students who hold themselves in high regard are happier and will succeed. Writing in *USA Today,* Sharon Jayson said that culture was so ingrained in parents that protecting their children from failure became a credo. Often-empty phrases ["good job"] raised a generation. Kids born in the 1970s and 1980s are now coming of age, and observers are watching them crumble a bit at the first blush of criticism," according to Jayson.

Now we've moved into the new century and there seems to be no single approach or "best" way to raise children. Diversity in ethnicity, beliefs, family structures, and family situations has allowed for the proliferation of diversity in ideas on how best to parent. Experts are no longer just medical, psychological, or educational professionals. Anyone who has direct experience with children can now be an "expert." Working moms, stay-at-home moms, ethnic moms, single moms, urban moms, celebrity moms, and even TV nannies now promote their own ideas on parenting. For every unique idea and approach, there is a mom looking for some answers on how to raise a healthy, happy child.

With so many new ideas offered on parenting, the one thing that is certain today, is that for the most part, today's moms and children seem to have become a closer entity—especially when it comes to what is most important to today's marketers—the decision-making process pertaining to purchasing certain goods and services.

Most importantly, we believe that the new mom and child relationship—what we call the four-eyed, four-legged consumer, leads to some important new understandings and rule changes when it comes to marketing goods and services in this new millennium. You can bet that we'll be talking about these throughout the rest of this book.

Some Implications

- When developing marketing plans targeting women, consider that they might also be moms. Look for ways in which to capitalize on this.

- With the absence of one key authority on parenting, many moms today are searching for tips on how to be better moms. Forms of marketing communications that also provide her with important mom tips might be very welcome here.

2

How Did This Happen?

TO FULLY UNDERSTAND the marketing implications of this new 4i4l consumer it is important to understand how and why this union between kid and mom has occurred. Many of these developments will be discussed in greater detail throughout the book.

How did this happen? Simply put, kids have changed, moms have changed, and mom's needs have changed. A new solution was inevitable.

There's a New Kid on the Block . . .

Today's kids are different from children just a few years ago. These differences have led them to being far more confident and informed when it comes to suggesting purchases to their moms.

• **They are computer influenced.** As we'll see throughout this book, computers have had a major impact on today's 4i4l consumer, not only from changing how they get and give information, but also how we as marketers must communicate to them and even how they, especially kids, actually process information. Eight of ten kids aged 6 to 11 now use computers at home and according to Home Depot's going-back-to-school research for 2005, 60 percent of today's parents think that a computer is the top priority for their children's success.

• **They are better educated.** Never underestimate the impact that computers and technology have and will have on kids' ability to learn more and learn faster. In 2001, passage of the No Child Left Behind Act set before our country the challenge to help every child achieve at higher levels. An important part of achieving this challenge has been to increase student access and ability on computers. In 2003, then Secretary of Education, Ron Paige stated: "By harnessing technology, we can expand access to learning and close the achievement gap." Now, from the back office to the classroom, schools are effectively employing technology to better meet the needs of today's students.

A study by NetDay in early 2003 found that fully 100 percent of teen students felt that the internet helped them with schoolwork. Fully 87 percent of these students ranked themselves as intermediate to expert in their use of the internet. Substantially more teens reported receiving mostly "A's" for their last report card than in the previous two years.

Students describing their last report card . . .

	May 2003	May 2002	May 2001
Mostly A's	32%	22%	20%
Mix of A's/B's	35	35	33
Mostly B's	7	8	8
Mix of B's/C's	19	23	26
C's/Below	7	12	13

SOURCE: *The State of Our Nation's Youth, 2003–2004,* Horatio Alger Foundation.

Today's youth are also being educated in social service. High schools are increasingly requiring community service experience for graduation. Interestingly, more than half of today's high schoolers actually endorse this idea and almost three quarters say that they do some sort of volunteering or community service, according to a report from the Horatio Alger Association.

Kids today are also becoming educated in business. From having to do Power Point presentations and working in "committees" in school, to being coached by parents on specific business practices, kids understand business. In July 2005, a *New York Times* article "Listen, Kid, You Have to Be Tough to Make it in This Business Today," author Julie Bick points out that even the lemonade stand has become an entrepreneurial venture for kids. The Junior Achievement Organization now has an internet student center, supplying sample business plans, videos, and even an online business game. Brad Kaufmann, a Junior Achievement spokesman was quoted in the article: "More kids are eager to learn real business skills at an earlier age, and their parents are right there to help them."

• **They have more to do.** Unlike their predecessors who were likely to be bored with free time, 70 percent of today's 6-to-11-year-olds like to have time on their own. In fact, almost one-third (30 percent) now say that they don't have enough free time according to Roper's *Youth Report,* nor do they feel they get enough privacy. The same probably holds true for today's teens, as they report spending more time on homework than ever before. Almost half (47 percent) of today's teens now report doing at least six hours a week of homework—up ten points versus just one year ago. Fourteen percent report doing ten hours or more of homework per week, according to the Horatio Alger Association.

Percent of 6-to-11-year-olds who strongly agree that they love	
Playing Sports	*60%*
Computer Time	*51*
Reading Books	*48*
SOURCE: Kid Simmons, Fall 2004	

And, when they do get some free time, what do today's kids do with it? Obviously, they have more to do than before thanks again to the computer. Computer time has become competitive with time previously split between playing sports and reading. The good news is that today's kids are pretty well rounded. While computer time has certainly become a major favorite pastime, playing sports is still the most favorite activity.

So, while the computer has given today's kids something to do while at home, it is encouraging to note that today's kids still are far from dormant. In fact, the 2004 Roper *Youth Report* shows an *increase* in health and fitness among kids, reporting that "the share of kids who exercised, jogged, or

Percent of 6-to-12-year-olds who played in past year	
Bicycling	*65%*
Swimming	*61*
In-Line Skating	*41*
Bowling	*41*
Basketball	*36*
Fishing	*35*
Soccer	*32*
Baseball/Softball	*32*
Dancing	*31*
Skateboarding	*23*
SOURCE: Kid Simmons, Fall 2004	

worked out in the past week is as high as it's been since first asked in 1997. According to *Sports Illustrated for Kids,* 64 percent of active tweens and young adults believe that being healthy and physically active is extremely important.

Tween & teen past year participation	
Basketball	74%
Football	65
Soccer	56
Jogging	55
Baseball	54
Swimming	49
Rollerblading	44

SOURCE: *Sports Illustrated for Kids*

When it comes to physical activity kids still participate in sports the way they've done for many years. Bicycling, swimming and skating are still prime activities among all young kids. Among older tweens and teens, basketball, football and soccer rank among the top.

• **There is much more media.** The media environment of today's youth is unquestionably different from that when their parents were growing up. Young people today have absolutely no fear when it comes to new technology. For perspective, more than half of today's 8-to-17-year-olds state that they find new technology "exciting and use it as much as I can." This compares with one-third of today's adults, according to Roper Reports.

But, what is most important is the fact that the media environment for today's kids is also dramatically different than it was for children of just five years ago. As detailed in a March 2005 Kaiser Family Foundation Study, "Decreases in the prices of personal computers, growing use of high-speed internet connections, developments in size and definition of TV screens, rapid diffusion of DVD players, the introduction of affordable digital TV recorders, the emergence of digital music recorders and music file-sharing" all took place in just the past five years. Children aged six months to six years are now spending as much time with TV, computers, and video games as they do playing outside.

To learn about current events, high schoolers today are actually more likely to turn to their televisions or computers than traditional news sources. But, despite their high levels of media use, they are now more skeptical about messages they receive through the media. Two in five students say that they have just some confidence in the media according to the NetDay study.

As a result, today's youth is exposed to an average of 8.5 hours of various media everyday—often using more than one medium at a time like TV and the internet, or radio and print. Many educators now think that this fast-paced media is having an effect on children's ability to concentrate, according to an article in *USA Today* by Marilyn Elias. One can only surmise that this is occurring not only in school but also with messages that marketers put to them.

• **They are smarter consumers.** Partly as a result of their internet savvy, partly from newer schooling methods that teach kids to look for truth or lies (because as teachers will tell their students, *anyone* can publish *anything* on the internet), partly because their moms are teaching them to be better consumers, today's kids are smarter consumers than were their predecessors of just five years ago. Today's kids will search the internet for more information, be more skeptical of false or misleading ad claims and, therefore be more confident in their choices and recommendations to parents. As the authors of the Roper *Youth Report* state: "American youth's approach to life is airborne by dreams and grounded by reality. In some ways they are expressing a more serious side, but they are doing so without losing their essential "kid-ness."

There is now evidence that as a result of today's kids having to multitask with so many media, their brains might be changing to enable them to juggle and concentrate better than their predecessors. Scores on intelligence tests have been steadily rising. These tests generally measure a child's ability to shift and divide attention as well as cover problem-solving and comprehension skills. Sam Goldstein, University of Utah neurophysiologist told *USA Today* (when talking about today's kids) "They're smarter."

The key to remember here is that because today's kids are learning more and faster they have become a much stronger, more educated consumer and a far more important partner to mom.

• **They are internet savvy.** Up until about a year ago, we were among the many kid marketing consultants warning our clients not to invest too heavily in the internet. The truth was, while some kids were going to the internet, there weren't that many kids doing it and those that did, did not stay on it long enough nor visit enough sites to warrant any significant marketing attention.

But over the past decade, we have seen the computer moving from the background of education to the forefront. Educators today are integrating the computer and the internet into school curricula making them prevalent in schools and lessons, according to Harris Interactive. This, in turn, has caused more parents to purchase computers and internet for their children at home. After all, no parent wants her child to lag behind others when it comes to education.

The fact is, today's kids are *very* comfortable with the internet, and they have become fully functional members of the "information age." For perspective, the study *Children, Families and the Internet* by Grunwald Associates, found that only about half of all kids aged 8 to12 used the internet as recently as the year 2000. Today that number has jumped considerably. Seventy-nine percent now report using the internet regularly from home *and* 45 percent of these do so with high-speed access, according to Roper Reports. In fact, just the other day, my 5-year-old granddaughter pointed to a tiny copyright notice under a SpongeBob picture on her drinking glass and automatically assumed it was his e-mail address. Then she told me that she never saw a website address like this one before!

What is especially important to marketers is the degree to which today's youth turns to the internet to obtain information on products and services—many times at the direction of their parents. And, again, these numbers are all up dramatically in just the past 2 years, according to Yankelovich *Youth Monitor.*

Percentage of schools with internet access

1995	50%
1996	65
1997	78
1998	89
1999	95
2000	98
2001	99

SOURCE: National Center for Education Statistics, internet Access in US Public Schools and Classrooms

---

Percent of online kids whose parents have asked them to use the internet to get product information

AGE

9 to 11	25%
12 to 14	45
15 to 17	65

SOURCE: "The Influence of Millennials," Yankelovich *Youth Monitor,* 2005

This newfound internet expertise, coupled with children's natural sense of curiosity and "ignorance" of what *can't* be done, has enabled them to find new ways to acquire information, new ways to communicate, and new ways to entertain themselves.

• **Their toys are different.** Today's kids have come to expect and require continued stimulation and this is certainly reinforced by the toys and games they play. Now kids happily play away at a Game Boy Advance, PlayStation2, not as much with traditional toys like board games, action figures, or puzzles. Once a little girl starts playing with GameBoy, it's harder to get her away and interested in dressing her Barbies. Heading into the end of 2004, the video game industry was looking at another record year, up about 7 percent, while traditional toy sales continued to slump, down about 5 percent.

NPD research reports that almost half of 4-to-5-year-olds are already playing video games and 20 percent of 3-year-olds are doing so too. Action figures, which were once sold to boys as old as 12, now top out at age 6. A recent survey by the consulting firm Funosophy found fewer than half of kids aged 6 to 8 preferred traditional toys to consumer electronics. This drops to fewer than 25 percent among tweens.

• **Kids are connected.** Thanks to buddy lists, cell phones and other soon-to-be-launched communication devices, kids today can and do spread the word to other kids faster and more than ever before. Twenty-two percent of today's kids now have the use of their own cell phones, according to Roper Reports. Most have up to 200 names on their buddy lists. Further, there is instant messaging (IM). A computer activity barely used by kids just five years ago, IM has emerged to become one of the most popular of all kid computer activities today, according to the Henry J. Kaiser Family Foundation.

The Kaiser Family Foundation states: "There are 36 million active screen names on AIM, and 25 percent are for users under 17," and "Two billion IMs fly through cyberspace every day—for all ages."

• **Kids demand more say.** New technology and the increased attention given to them by today's marketers have caused children to now expect far more attention and participation than ever before. Thanks again to the internet, kids now have a voice where they have never had one before. For example, Nickelodeon Network asks them on a daily basis, to vote on various topics via the internet. Also, the annual Nick Choice Awards, where kids are asked to vote on their favorite stars is now one of the most sought after tickets in the business. For the 2005 Kids Choice Awards, over 18 million votes were tallied online, including 200,000 "live" votes for Best Hidden Talent. On the day of the show itself, *Nick.com* attracted nearly 700,000 unique visitors. Even one of our own promotions for a client, asking kids to vote for one meal over another garnered tens of thousands of internet votes from children as young as age 3.

• **They are consensual.** Most important, consistent with the identification of our 4i4l consumer, today's kids are much more prone to working things out with their parents. In fact, the 2004 Roper *Youth Report* calls the kid of today the "Consensual Kid," and states conclusively "this is a different group than kids of a decade ago."

As we will soon see with today's moms, kids today show that "family" is even more important to them than it was to their predecessors. Almost three out of four kids agree that they regularly discuss the good things in life with their parents and this holds true for kids from age 6 to age 17. Kids of all ages report doing more with families today versus kids five years ago, according to Yankelovich.

Activities you usually/sometimes do with your family

	AGED 6 TO 11		AGED 12 TO 14		AGED 15 TO 17	
		2003 vs. 1997		2003 vs. 1997		2003 vs. 1997
Movies	*90%*	*+4*	*85%*	*+67*	*4%*	*+8*
Outdoor activities	*74*	*+13*	*73*	*+10*	*67*	*+18*
Cards/board games	*NA*	*NA*	*80*	*+8*	*68*	*+16*
Video games	*61*	*+5*	*58*	*+7*	*47*	*+7*
Play online/computer	*53*	*+20*	*51*	*+13*	*48*	*+12*

SOURCE: "The Influence of Millennials," Yankelovich *Youth Monitor,* 2005

PLUS . . . There is a New Mom in the House!

The finding that kids today are different than those of just a few years ago is only half of the story, because today's moms also bear little resemblance to their predecessors. From the tattoos on their bodies (32 percent of GenX moms have these) to their heavy reliance on the web and their active partnering with their kids, these aren't the moms you thought you knew!

Signs everywhere point to an undeniable conclusion that motherhood has experienced some radical changes. Motherhood is no longer primarily the role of Baby Boomers. As stated in the "Who's Your Momma?" article which appeared in *Advertising & Marketing to Children in* July 2004, "We are currently at the crossroads of a generational torch-passing from Baby Boomer moms to GenX and GenY." In 2005, only about one-third of *all* moms of today's kids aged 0 to 17 are Boomers, but the *average* mother is a GenXer. GenXers were born from 1965–1976 (some say 1979), making them about 30 to 40 years of age today. With the average age of first-time moms now almost 25 years of age, we see that typically children aged 5 to 15 can now call their mothers "Madam X."

> The day of the Boomer Mom is over and marketers must take notice of the differences between yesterday's mom and the new generation.
>
> —SABRINA NEELEY AND TIM COFFEY
>
> SOURCE: "Who's Your Momma?" *Advertising and Marketing to Children,* July–September 2004.

The fact that moms today are composed largely of GenXers (and even some GenYers) as opposed to Baby Boomers has far more ramifications than simply playing a game of Alphabet! Let's understand why and how today's moms became so different.

It's been said that experience is the toughest teacher; first you get the test, then you get the lesson. And, one need only look at the experiences that today's GenXers had in their formative years to understand why their approaches and attitudes toward motherhood and consumerism are so different from those of their predecessors.

• **Baby Boomer parents**. Today's moms are the first moms ever to have had parents that were, unfortunately, largely consumed with themselves, not their children nor their families. Douglas Adams of Appel Associates, points out that "today's GenX moms were born during one of the most blatantly anti-child phases in history." Abortion and birth control were considered by many to be preferable to having children. Kids were viewed as intrusive obstacles to their parent's self-exploration.

• **The ERA**. Just when today's earliest GenXer was toddling around the house, her mom was becoming pressed by her peers with the *need* and the *duty* to put much, if not all, of her attention on becoming a successful, achieving working woman. In 1967, the National Organization for Women (NOW) was founded, pledging to fight tirelessly for the ratification of the Equal Rights Amendment.

NOW's highly visible political fighting over ratification of the ERA helped to keep it a top women's issue throughout the entire GenX era. The GenXer's mom, the Boomer, felt more and more reason, if not pressure, to "prove herself" in the work force as the ERA continued to gain Congressional approval and then state-by-state ratification, until, then-presidential-candidate Ronald Regan actively opposed it in mid-1980—almost to the day the youngest GenXer started kindergarten!

• **Education**. Unlike her Boomer mom, who for the most part, began learning from her earliest childhood educational years the value of "home economics," or if she *was* looking for a major career, perhaps being a "secretary or maybe, just maybe, a "nurse" or "dental hygienist," today's mom was blessed with seeing the alternative of higher education and career choice in her earliest school years. She was introduced to the possibility of becoming a cellular biologist, business executive, lawyer, doctor, and more.

As a result of better preparation in early schooling and possibly some heavy coaxing from her success-oriented Boomer parents, today's GenX mom was far more likely to go on to college. More than 50 percent of today's GenX moms attended at least some college and, in

2001, accounted for 41 percent of all MBAs, 43 percent of all medical degrees and 47 percent of all law degrees, according to a *Time Magazine* article by Claudia Walling.

• **In-school sports.** Thanks in part to the governmental edict for equal sports opportunities for girls and boys in school, today's GenX mom was far more likely to be exposed to the benefits of sports participation than was her mom. Studies of child development have often brought up the benefits that sports participation adds to the development of the male psyche—leadership, confidence, group or team dynamics, and competitiveness. Now, for the first time, those benefits were becoming largely available to GenX girls.

• **Home alone.** With moms and dads who were often consumed with advancing their personal careers and embracing other forms of self-gratification, many of today's moms became part of the most unsupervised generation in history, finding themselves home alone much too often. Unlike her mom before her, today's mom often did not have a stay-at-home mom to watch over her in the afternoon, or let her roam freely around the neighborhood. Nor was she as likely to have a brother or sister to keep her company. Rather, she was the first of the "latch-key" kids.

As a result, as a child, today's mom had to depend more on mental or passive activities. Her TV and telephone became her best companions. Many believe that because of the absence of her parents, the primary influencer on the life of today's GenX mom was her TV. And what was she watching? She was watching TV shows that worshiped the value of strong, loving families! According to Rob Owen, author of *Gen X TV*, the number one show viewed by the GenX latchkey kid was *The Brady Bunch*! Also among the top five were *Happy Days, Family Ties,* and *Little House on the Prairie.* (*Love Boat* was the only exception to this top 5 fact.)

• **Family instability.** Sadly, mom of today became all too aware that the line "till death do you part" really had to do more with funerals than with marriages. More than one of every two moms today saw her own family split by divorce while she was a child, and virtually all of today's moms knew of at least some close friends whose families were being broken up through divorce.

• TV/MTV. This is *the* MTV generation. Unlike their moms, who grew up with, at best, TV with a choice of just three networks, the GenXer was the first generation to see TV explode. In the late 1970s, when the oldest GenX mom was entering her teen years, TV erupted with the start of cable. And by 1981, when today's youngest GenX mom was not even in kindergarten, MTV was born. No wonder the moms of today seem to be more appreciative and critical about music and graphics surrounding advertising.

• Marketing to kids. Right in the heart of today's GenX mom's early formative years, yet another phenomenon occurred—Marketing to Kids! While marketing to kids certainly did not begin during this generation's formative years, it undoubtedly did hit new, previously unheard of levels. Boomer kids had *some* advertising and promotions targeted to them, but it was basically only the most rudimentary candy, toy, cereal, or an occasional beverage product advertisement. And this was being delivered on only the few TV channels existing back then.

But in the mid-1980s marketers began to truly wake up to the huge influence and purchasing power of this generation of children. And POW, here came the beginning of a plethora of products, services, and advertising targeted directly toward them and coming to them from the new cable and network stations—new networks like FOX, which first came into existence when today's average GenX mom became a tween.

• Technology. Right in the middle of the GenXer mom's most formative years (1980s), personal computers, Walkmans and video recorders were becoming the norm. Unlike her predecessor mom, handcuffed with the previously considered "modern" electric typewriter, GenX mom was being trained on and was growing up with the PC and all that it could do.

In fact, when today's average mom was only 12 years of age, AOL was already beginning to mass-mail its "Getting America Online" disks. By the time she was a teen, readying herself for college, the internet and access to greater information was becoming mainstream.

No longer the slave to having to listen to or watch whatever was on the radio or TV at the same time as her mom did, today's moms grew up with having power and control over their music and video environment.

• **The economy.** While she saw her parents working hard to achieve everything materially desirable, today's mom also saw what can happen if you just blindly trust the economy. GenX moms all witnessed the late 1980s recession triggered in 1987 by the collapse of the American savings and loan corporations. Black Monday, October 1987, saw the largest single day drop ever in the Dow Jones (25 percent), putting what many felt was their lifetime savings and pensions in jeopardy.

• **AIDS.** For final measure, just in case today's GenX moms felt the desire to follow in their parent's footsteps when it came to carefree sex, along came HIV/AIDS. Unlike her Baby Boom parents, who were at least, in the press, likely to be enjoying musical beds, swinging parties, and multiple sex partners while dissolving their marriages, these new moms learned there was a price to pay. Just when many were reaching puberty, headlines began featuring celebrity deaths from AIDS.

These are just some of the experiences today's moms have gone through during their formative years, years and experiences that taught them the lessons they would now use, as they became parents of today's kids.

So . . . What's She Like?

Thanks in part to these and other experiences, what are today's moms like? Well, most (63 percent) report that they are happy with their lives as is, but, hey, this sure isn't everyone, according to Fall 2004 Simmons data.

• **Family and motherhood are important.** It wasn't too long ago that moms felt a strong connection to the words and music of the Enjoli (perfume) commercial:

> *Woman:* I can put the wash on the line, feed the kids, get dressed, pass out the kisses, and get to work by five of nine.
>
> *Chorus:* 'Cause I'm a woman . . . (Enjoli!)
>
> *Woman:* I can bring home the bacon (Enjoli!), fry it up in a pan (Enjoli!), and never, never, never forget you're a man (Enjoli!). 'Cause I'm a woman . . . (Enjoli!)

Not now. They're not Boomer moms. While Boomers are more likely to be work-centric, GenXers are more likely to be dual-centric or family-centric. It's no wonder that after declining sharply from 1970 to 1995, the number of families headed by married couples began to stabilize at about 68 percent around 1996.

Today's GenX mom has seen the good and also the bad of being a Boomer-type of mom, and they're having none of it! In a Spring, 2003 CLUB Mom Survey, 70 percent of young moms stated that they spend more time with their children than their moms spent with them; 40 percent said *much* more time. In short, today's mom wants to be a great mom! In fact, unlike her Boomer mom, today's mom is selfless—preferring to think of herself *after* her children.

Relative priority placed on work versus family, 2002		
Work Centric	Dual Centric	Family Centric
GenX 13%	35%	52%
Boomer 22	37	41
Matures 12	54	34

SOURCE: "Generation and Gender in the Workplace," Families and Work Institute.

Whether this is all the result of their past experiences or special change events such as the developments of 9/11, the thing that matters most to today's moms is not how to best clean their dishes, wash the clothes, or make the best meals. Rather it is to build close relationships with their children, expanding their horizons and setting the stage for their kids to live happy lives, according to Maria Bailey, author of *Marketing to Moms*.

A 2005 *Motherhood Study* commissioned by the University of Minnesota and the University of Connecticut Institute for American

Values found that regardless of age, race, ethnicity, religious affiliation, geography, or employment status, moms agree in their perceptions of the importance of mothering. Eighty-one percent of mothers said that mothering is the most important thing they do and 93 percent said that the love they feel for their children is unlike any other love the have experienced. As one mom put it:

> I want to say this without tearing up—my kids are my life. They are my angels. I wouldn't change whatever I have to go through with them for anything in this world.

Today's moms actually celebrate motherhood. Just look at some of the belly-baring maternity fashions now featured in the fashion ads. Look at the covers of *People, Cosmo,* and other magazines featuring women who are pregnant and proud.

When *Clubmom.com* asked its panel in 2002, "What are your priorities as a mom or a prospective mom?" the number one answer was: "To enable happiness and joy." This was further described as: Spending time with their children, teaching them morals and values, and giving them unconditional love.

And, today's newer mom seems to be even more into her children than the average mom. A 2000 *New Mother Market Study* by the Parenting Group found that today's newest mothers were even more likely to be into their children and motherhood roles compared with all moms of kids under age 12.

Family is far more important to her than her boomer predecessor. Simmons Research found that 89 percent of today's moms agreed that they enjoy spending time with their families. Research by Catalyst, New York, found that 86 percent of today's GenX women say that having a loving family is extremely important.

Consistent with the importance that this mom places on family, she is more likely to stay at home with her children and those that continue working largely do so for economic reasons. Forty-five percent of moms with infants do not work, up from 41 percent in 1998. One in four moms in their prime career years of 25 to 44 are now staying home with their children full-time. Of those moms that do work, only one in three work a 40-hour work week and many of these do so only because of divorce, separation or widowhood. Reportedly, about half of those that work full time would rather work only part time and most women still desire to work in some manner, but would prefer more flexible arrangements, according to the 2005 *Motherhood Study* cited earlier

As such, the 75 percent of women that must work to some extent report valuing their family time more than their parents did and, they are persuading their employers to understand and do something about it. Even as little as four years ago, only 30 percent of companies of the 100 best list offered a variety of childcare and flexibility options; now most companies do, according to *Working Mother.* In the 2005 *Motherhood Study*, 83 percent of moms surveyed gave their employers credit for trying to accommodate their motherhood needs—allowing them to bring their children to work when the need arises; letting them take extra time off for childcare; allowing them to work from home or being flexible about hours.

Unlike the pressure felt by stay-at-home moms during the Boomer mom years, there are no longer the "mommy wars"—the tension that was observed even a few years ago between mothers who were employed outside the home and those who were not. Whether employed outside of the home or not, many moms want a middle ground when it comes to work—one that lets them feel the productivity and satisfaction of work but also gives them the flexibility and time to excel as mothers.

Today's moms saw too many broken families in their childhood and they want none of it for their families and children. Therefore, they are highly protective of them.

According to an April 2004 *USA Today* article by Karen Peterson, for Boomers, working was high status but now, for GenX, not working outside of home is considered the new status symbol.

• **She wants to do it ALL!** But being a great mom isn't enough for today's GenXers. Because of her superior education, mom today still wants a rewarding career. While Boomer moms blazed a trail for work and careers, GenX moms strive for much more balance in their lives—trying to be both good workers and great moms. In fact about two-thirds of today's moms agree that it is important for them to juggle various tasks, according to Simmons data.

Also, because the GenX mom of today does not want to end up divorced or debt ridden like her parents, she strives for a sense of purpose and balance in her work and home life.

Unfortunately, trying to do it all and striving for a work and home life balance has not come easily for our moms. While children of GenX parents have received more attention than children of Baby Boomer parents, there is no significant difference between the number of hours, paid and unpaid, worked per week by GenX workers versus their Boomer counterparts over 25 years ago, according to *Research Alert*.

It seems odd that whereas GenXers desire so much to be more family/dual centric than their Boomer work-centric parents were, they actually work longer hours. In fact, combined work hours for dual-earner couples with children rose 10 hours a week, from 81 hours in 1977, to 91 hours a week today, according to the *National Study of the Changing Workforce*.

So guess where this extra child time is coming from? Yup, personal time. Sure, dads have helped. Over the past 25 years, dads have given up an additional 48 minutes a day in time spent for themselves, leaving them with only 1.3 hours of personal time per day. But moms have virtually matched this and now have *a luxurious 54 minutes* a day left for themselves, the *National Study of the Changing Workforce* reports.

We will revisit this in even greater detail when we discuss "stress" later in the chapter.

• She is smart. Since more than half of today's GenX women are college educated, it is not surprising that they now hold more than half of all executive, administrative, and managerial occupations. Today's moms rate themselves as smart, bright and well informed and see themselves as diligent and thorough. More than 80 percent of all moms feel that it is important to continue learning new things and that it is important to be well informed, according to Simmons.

As such, she certainly knows where to go to get the information she needs regarding any purchase decisions needing to be made. For perspective, when it comes to health issues, Simmons finds that one-third of today's moms will actually research treatments on her own before asking her doctor. Our own research confirms that moms today are comfortable in actually suggesting medication for their physicians to prescribe. Even some pediatricians are reportedly not suggesting particular formulas for first-time moms, but rather are encouraging them to make their own decisions. Of course, with this greater intelligence together with her better information-finding skills honed on the internet, she strongly disdains the hard-sell techniques of the past.

• **She is independent.** Since the mom of today tended to be brought up alone with less family and sibling interaction, she herself has become fiercely independent. According to Simmons data, the majority of GenX moms of today see themselves as self assured and confident (56 percent). Almost half (45 percent) report that they see themselves as brave and courageous. She doesn't trust others (aka "marketers"!).

Who does she value? Friends! She values and relies on friendships. No wonder that the sitcom *Friends* was so popular. She also trusts *herself* and will make up her own mind. She also values work, but not for money, rather for a career—and for security because, again, she has learned from her prior experiences with divorced parents not to trust her husband's income.

One of the most surprising numbers confirming this new mom's independence is the fact that today, one-third of all births are to single moms—double over 10 years ago.

• **She expects herself and her children to succeed and achieve.** She's been to college so she expects her children to do the same. In fact, because of her education, she values education even more. As a result, she'll make certain her children get all of the head starts they can, such as PBS television, and Leap Frog Learning Systems. Having absorbed the findings of recent studies showing that the first few years of a child's life offer the best opportunities for learning, she is sending her children off to pre-kindergarten at historical rates. The Census Bureau reports that in 2003, almost 60 percent of all eligible children were enrolled in preschool—more than double the percentage of the Boomer mom era.

In fact, according to Simmons research, GenXers start saving for their children's college educations when their children are just two and a half years of age compared with older than seven years of age for Boomer parents. And 68 percent of GenX parents are now saving for their kids' college education—more than double the number for older parents.

Consistent with her desire to make sure that her children succeed, she will make sure that her children are ready to be *educated consumers*. So, as mentioned in Chapter 1, it is not unusual to find her actually encouraging her young children to make choices when they're with her in the supermarket.

> I encourage my child to go shopping with me so she can learn how purchases are chosen, how to compare items, how to get a good deal, etc., so she can be an informed consumer about her purchases both now and when she will make most of her own purchases.
>
> MOM OF GIRL AGED 8 TO 11
>
> SOURCE: *WonderGroup Mom/Kid Influence Study*

• **She is visually stimulated.** Since the GenX mom is truly the first of the TV/MTV generation, she is extraordinarily comfortable with, and even critical of, visual stimulation. Today's MTV graduate has a propensity for the loud graphics, quick edits, severe camera angles that were probably impossible, or certainly unpleasant for her parents to follow. Probably never before has the phrase, "a picture is worth a thousand words," been more accurate. In fact, recently, we observed new moms evaluating various Evenflo print ads for communications and effectiveness in focus groups. All of a sudden the women began talking about the quality of the photo, the simplicity of the look, even the type style. Art directors are loving it!

• **She is internet savvy.** She was the first to have had computers in class. She was there for the birth of AOL. Some used and depended on the internet while in college. So, she is comfortable relying on the internet for information regarding purchases. According to Simmons' 2005 research, over 50 percent of today's moms report going to the internet prior to making any significant purchases. In many cases she is also relying on the internet to discuss various topics, including products, with others.

• **She has marketing savvy.** Unlike her Boomer predecessor, this mom was heavily marketed and advertised to as a child. She is quite knowledgeable about the truths and sometimes half-truths of advertising. She has learned that those wonderful prizes that you just might win if you compose and send in a 1,000 word essay, plus send in a color picture, plus even promise never ever to be bad, were prizes that hardly anyone ever won. Because of this, she is likely to help her children better understand and cope with the marketing being aimed at them. But even more important, she knows that marketing *to them* is not such a bad thing to do. In fact, she knows that it can actually help her children become smart consumers, not to mention that it can also make her life a little easier. After all, it sure didn't hurt her!

• **She is having children later in life.** Partly as a result of a drop in teen pregnancies, partly due to wanting a career first, partly due to wanting to finish educations and balance their desires for career with desires of having a family, the average age of today's mom is 27.2 years of age—up one full year versus 1990; two from 1980 according to the U.S. Census Bureau. Thirty-five percent of all births are to moms aged 30 to 39 and the average age for having a first baby is now 24.9 years.

• **Far more ethnic diversity.** There are now significant differences in birthrates by ethnicity. In fact about one-fourth of today's pregnant moms are Hispanic. And when compared to the population in general, we find among today's 18-to-34-year-olds:

  • 22 percent more likely to be Black
  • 15 percent more likely to be Asian
  • 59 percent more likely to be Hispanic

And Now—the Drawbacks!

The big need: time, money & simplicity!

There are lots of implications that you can draw about this new mom but perhaps, for marketers the biggest implication comes from what today's mom *feels!*

Since today's mom attempts to do it all, she can feel under tremendous stress at times. It's no wonder that 34 percent of moms with kids aged 4 and younger and 31 percent of moms with kids aged 4 to 17 report feeling stress "quite often—almost every day." This compares with only 19 percent of the total public, according to Roper Reports.

In particular, time and money have become especially precious commodities to her. More than half (54 percent) are unhappy with their current standard of living, according to Simmons, and many feel that they are now working especially hard in order to enjoy significant quality time with their children, something their parents often did not do for them.

The balancing act between motherhood and expectations has been a particularly tough one. Remember, the education, electronic media, and magazines that today's mom consumed in her formative years taught her to be a winner and gave her a general feeling of optimism. In her February 2005 *Newsweek* article on "Mommy Madness," Judith Warner reminds us that "even the most traditional women's magazines throughout the 1980s taught that the future for up-and-coming mothers was bright . . . work and motherhood *could* be balanced. It was all a question of intelligent juggling." Yet, as she points out later in her article, "there was *no way to make this most basic of balancing acts work.*"

The balancing act between motherhood and career, while highly desirable, has been even more difficult. Mom continues to be faced with the choice of either pursuing the professional dreams she acquired through her education at the cost of abandoning her children to childcare. Or she can stay at home with her children, feeling isolated, strapped for cash, and intellectually starved. According to James Chung, President of Reach Advisors, only 25 percent of GenX moms feel okay about their work-and-life balance. Interestingly, this is significantly down from the 35 percent of Boomer moms who reported being happy despite spending less time with their children!

Since she is trying to do so much more with her time and money, value has become virtually mandatory for her. The financial pressure that moms feel is not the need to "keep up with the Joneses" but rather to save for their children's college expenses and to maintain their families' current lifestyle. In fact, while Boomers liked to talk about how much they spend, GenXers like to talk about how much they save. Fifty-five percent of today's moms state that they hold off on buying things until they go on sale and 69 percent state that they always look out for special offers, according to Simmons.

Yet, debt is still preferable to today's moms versus going back to the workforce. Rather, they continue to try to pare down their expenses.

Rather than buying the luxury goods that Boomers craved, GenXers are making trade-offs in order to spend more time with the family.

While today's GenX women have closed the pay gap versus men in the last 20 years, estimates still show them lagging well behind, achieving pay of anywhere from 69 percent to 82 percent of that reported for men, so they definitely still feel the pinch. And remember, staying home even a little, creates a further cash crunch.

Time also seems to be a very different commodity for moms than it is for other women. In mom focus groups on various promotional offers we saw an eye-opening example of how time crunched today's moms are. For example, one specific tried and true promotion offered a "money-back" guarantee if not totally satisfied. A surprisingly large number of moms voted this one down because it would require them to take time if they took the steps to exercise this right. As one mom told us:

It's not that I don't want to take the time; it's that the time is not there!

Mom can't help but feel that she's losing the time battle (at least a little bit) and she can sure use some help. (Hello marketers!)

The challenges of her battle to find balance in her life have also affected mom's ability to exercise and be healthy. The majority of today's moms report to be at least *trying* to be healthy, agreeing that they should exercise more, work at eating well-balanced diets, and try to eat healthier foods. In fact, almost one-third report that they are currently dieting. However, with less and less spare time, it has become increasingly difficult for them to keep fit, exercise or manage stress. The data suggests some of this difficulty.

Percent of moms who agree with statements:	
Should exercise more	71%
Try to eat healthy foods	62
Work at eating a balanced diet	55
Do at least some exercise	50
Am currently dieting	32

Percent of moms who also agree with statements:	
Eat foods I like regardless of calories	64%
Nothing wrong indulging in fattening foods	59
Too busy to take care of myself	46
Treat myself to foods not good for me	47

SOURCE: Simmons Research

So, how does mom today try to achieve this balance? One way is through flexibility in handling her work at home, through such devices as cell phones, laptops, BlackBerries, and the internet. She also tries to gain flexibility at work. According to a survey by the Families and Work Institute in New York, on a scale of 1 to 10 (with 10 most valued) employed mothers gave flexibility a 9.2 and advancement only a 5.5 when asked to rate how important each was for their job satisfaction.

Yet another form of flexibility is through the "flex-career," whereby mom takes some time out of the workforce when her children are young, and then returns later. In its latest study of the *Changing Workforce,* the Families and Work Institute found that 28 percent of women, who don't yet have children, were planning to leave the workforce for a period of time when they had children.

But an even more important way in which mom tries to achieve some balance in her life is through seeking simplicity. She wants help in making her job as mom to be as simple as possible. The last thing she wants is to waste her time (or her money)! She doesn't want to spend time shopping for, cooking, or making items that she then has to spend even more time trying to persuade her children to use. She doesn't want to spend time or money "guessing" what her children may or may not like. She'd rather know for sure.

> I definitely would not buy something if there is no way I could get her near it; my budget is not that big.
>
> MOM OF GIRL AGED 2 TO 4

> If I buy something that he won't eat or wear, it goes to waste.
>
> MOM OF BOY AGED 2 TO 4

> I don't want to waste money on stuff my daughter does not like, so it is important what she thinks.
>
> MOM OF GIRL AGED 5 TO 7

And how does a mom like this find simplification? Since today's mom has to do so much, she can't help at times to relax the rules and give in to the need for peace and convenience. Simmons finds that almost 4 in 10 agree that it is difficult to say no to her kids. According to *Parenting* magazine (June–July 2003):

- About 40 percent of moms admit that their children ate no green vegetables the night before or that they allowed their children dessert without having to finish dinner.

- Over half admit that family dinner is *not* a nightly occasion.

- More than a third bribe their children with treats in order to get them to eat.

One of our focus group moms put it clearly into perspective for us when she said: "I'm bad, but I'm not double-chocolate bad!"

However, mom is certainly not a pushover for her kids' desires. Rather she seems to have a balanced approach when it comes to raising her children. While many moms are permissive in the ways they allow their children to express themselves and in what they would like to provide for their children, they are not agreeing with everything their children want. The majority clearly feel that they have little difficulty telling their children "no." And, this ability by many to be at least somewhat restrictive will play out later in this book.

Moms' attitudes regarding children
(percent of moms agreeing)

Children should be allowed to express themselves	*61%*
Want to provide my kids with things I didn't have	*66*
Want to indulge my kids with little extras	*68*
Yet:	
Do not find it difficult to say no my kids	*63*
Believe kids are exposed to too much materialism	*75*

SOURCE: Simmons Research

The Inevitable Result

Add the components: Stressed, time-starved, educated mom looking for simplification **+** educated, market-savvy, more consensual kid **=**

THE PERFECT PARTNERSHIP! They have become one—the 4i4l!

A huge way that today's moms have tried to simplify their lives is by creating a oneness with their children. She'll rely on her child's recommendations and influence and she'll involve him or her as a partner rather than an adversary. The last thing she needs is to *waste* money, time, or even more important, her strength in buying items that her child won't want to use! Believe us, we have heard scores and scores of moms in focus groups requesting that pharmaceutical companies do a better job in helping them get their children to take necessary medications or asking cereal companies not to create such healthy cereals that their children won't eat breakfast. In fact in the latest Yankelovich *Youth Monitor,* 70 percent of moms agreed that it made their shopping easier when they knew particular brands that their children wanted.

And remember, mom has a great kid to partner with. Not only are today's kids smarter and even more savvy about marketing, but they are also consensual. Perhaps it is because today's kids feel more important as family members that they feel their family is more important to them. The percentage of kids saying they now need to check with a parent before making a purchasing decision has raised an average of 9 points in 2004 compared with 2001. About as many kids now report needing Mom (or Dad's) agreement as report making the decision themselves.

Percent of 8-to-17-year-olds saying they need to check with parent before purchasing

	Percent	Percent of change from 2001
Video Games	47%	+15
Video/DVD rentals	54	+14
CDs/Music	49	+12
Games/Toys	45	+12
Computer Software	37	+11
Books	37	+10
Personal Care	24	+10
Soft Drinks	25	+ 9

SOURCE: "The Consensual Kid," Roper Reports, 2004

And as a result, kids' activities and discussions with parents are on the rise. For example, the percentage of 4-to-17-year-olds reporting that they often discuss subjects with their parents is up at least 4 points from 2002 levels on at least half of sixteen issues. Among these issues, "how to spend money" is up 9 points, according to Roper Reports.

According to three-quarters of kids aged 6 to 14, their reliance on mom's advice lasts into the teen and young-adult years. In fact, teens cite moms as their top source of advice especially on family issues, career, and education. Younger kids value their moms for giving them support and encouragement, homework help, and other project help, according to EPM's *Marketing to Women*.

Consistent with this, the 2003–2004 edition of the Horatio Alger Association's "State of Our Nation's Youth" found that the families of high school students are now stronger than ever. Three-quarters of all students reported that they get along with their parents very well, or even better. When asked to pick the one or two areas of their life in which they would like to spend more time, half of today's students say they would like to spend more time with their families.

The ultimate result of this new partnership is that, in general, despite the strain and stress of being a mom today, mothers report high levels of satisfaction with their lives as mothers. The Institute for American Values 2005 *Motherhood Study* finds 81 percent of moms feeling very satisfied and 16 percent somewhat satisfied with their lives.

Moms of Tomorrow?

The new moms of tomorrow will be the GenYers. Right now, they are optimistic about the future. In fact, after September 11th, several more years of terrorist attacks abroad, troubles with the economy, and the war in Iraq, 75 percent of our future moms, today's high school students, look toward America's future with optimism. Half say that they have great confidence in the federal government, compared with only 34 percent of today's adults, according to the Horatio Alger Foundation.

Every indication is that this generation of moms will be at least similar in its desire to balance work and family and be as family oriented as their GenX counterparts. GenYers appear to want to make it an even greater priority to be a successful mom and have a great family. Some of this is already evident when you compare the percentage of today's moms with younger children (under 4), versus mothers with older children, who express their personal idea of success as being a good spouse/mother (68 percent vs. 59 percent), as found by Roper Reports.

Tomorrow's moms will be even savvier with technology and will be even better educated. Eighty-eight percent of today's teenagers think that they will go to college, and this is continuing to rise, up 8 points in just the past year, Roper finds. There will no doubt be more time management and multitasking technological advancements introduced into her world to make this goal even more achievable for her than ever before.

And there will be more of them! From 2000 to 2015, there will be a 17 percent increase in women falling into the prime child-bearing years, indicating the potential of 600,000 additional births per year—mirroring a rate last seen during the Baby Boom.

Some Implications

- Computers and technology are now so much a part of the youth's world that products, promotions, and even advertising that does not take advantage of this, or at least reflect it, could brand a marketer as "old fashioned."

- Kids today are far less likely to be bored. So when offering something new to this market, you must be sure that it is good enough to replace something else the kids are now doing. Just because it's new and fun may not be good enough!

- Kids today are savvier in business. Marketers must respect them and not try to fool them.

- Today's youth are tech savvy, smart, and know how to use the internet to search for the information they want. Marketers should make sure that they provide adequate information concerning their offerings on the internet.

- Interest has passed from traditional, static toys to more technological, interactive objects. Marketers need to look at incorporating technology and other interactive possibilities in their currently static marketing elements, like packages, ads and even the product, itself.

- Offer more items that help keep children involved, quiet, and in control throughout the day (so mom can do her other chores too). Educators can argue all they want about the dangers and drawbacks of video games, but today's moms still buy them. Why? Because they keep their children busy.

- Provide even more technology that allows moms to gain flexibility. Any item that allows her to easily access information, about her work, children, or life in general will be welcomed. No longer is just the internet important to moms. Wireless is even more important, so mom can access information from anywhere, including the laundry room!

- Have an up-to-date internet strategy. Mom is internet savvy, so help her to find you and enable her to easily access as much information as she wants. Shame on those who do not provide internet support!

- Recognize mom's comfort with visuals. Marketers should communicate and entice with visuals and avoid trying to tell her everything you want to. Rather, provide verbal or written information where she can find it if and when she wants to.

- Help mom to help her children succeed. Fun-to-learn programs and easy-to-teach exercises will continue to interest her.

- Remember, mom's world is largely her children. Offer mom experiences and pastimes for just her and her child—day trips and exercises, that she alone (or with her friends) can enjoy with her children. We have seen particularly strong concept scores from moms on products or activities that allow them to do something together with their children.

- Today's moms are smarter and more educated than ever before. Communicate to them in an educated manner. Avoid the "hard sell" exaggerations that she will see as insulting to her intelligence.

- Keep products technologically up to date. She is technologically savvy and if your product is not, she'll see it as boring and old fashioned. For example, in a recent product test of some new children's educational materials, moms quickly panned them for not having CDs!

- Make promotional offers and even purchasing opportunities easy to accomplish. Many moms don't have the time to take any extra steps.

- Marketers should not only help mom save time overall, but break down larger tasks into manageable chunks, breaking tasks like cooking, playing, and paying bills, into 10–15 minute chunks.

- Marketers should take advantage of today's kids seeking consensus from mom on such topics as education and career among other things, and making sure that moms as well as kids receive information on these topics.

- Most moms will have to work at some time and the workplace will change. Moms will continue to look for flexibility, and technology will enable workplaces to offer that flexibility. New home and on-the-go workstations, and equipment, will flourish.

- Remember, it has become difficult for moms to strike a balance between the needs of their children, their own needs, and getting everything else done. Marketers must be sensitive to this and not talk to her like she has it all under control. She doesn't!

- Assume all moms have very busy lives and that most will be in the labor force at some time during their parenting years.

- Moms find feeling attractive and having the time and energy for personal care to be challenging, so recognize that the woman in mom needs attention and support too.

- Find ways to market to moms during their waiting times, such as when they are in lines at the bank, or at the store, or at the pediatrician's office.

- Financial services should be positioned as contributing to mom's long-term goals (college educations for her kids, for example) rather than enabling an affluent lifestyle.

3

Life Stages of the Four-Eyed, Four-Legged Consumer

THE NATURE OF THE Four-Eyed, Four-Legged Consumer, referred to from now on as 4i4l, changes as the child matures from pregnancy to teen. We've already discussed how today's moms, and therefore their children, are substantially different than the previous generations in their approach to life and parenting in particular. So building on that generational perspective, we will now take a more vertical look at the 4i4l consumer. By examining their life stages, we can better understand how the 4i4l develops and changes over time. Each stage of the 4i4l brings a new relationship between mother and child that significantly affects the mode and nature of how they make decisions together, each stage informing the next. And, most importantly, each stage requires a different approach for effectively marketing to the 4i4l consumer.

In relationship terms we see three stages—Dependence, Conditional, and Interdependence—which emerge over the life stages of the mother and child. Each stage is characterized by a different mix and balance of mutual decision-making styles. For the past several decades, the view of this decision-making relationship has been characterized as a nagging child, whining, pestering, and cajoling her parent to get what she wants, with the parent (mostly mom) represented as the "gatekeeper" who decides which requests are granted. While we are not saying that there is no truth in these characterizations, we have seen in our own and others' research that there is much more to the story.

The "rest of the story" identifies a different view of how mom and kid navigate the aisles of consumerism that reveals far more collaboration than once believed, as both mom and kid simultaneously seek to meet their respective needs. The concept of "teamwork" was identified in an article in the *Journal of Advertising Research* by Dr. Langbourne Rust, which found that "parent interactions with older children often reflected a degree of teamwork: a division of labor with coordination and communication between members of the shopping party and a set of shared objectives." In our 2005 *Mom/Kid Influence Study,* we found clear evidence of this more collaborative relationship even among moms and children aged 2 to 4 that increases as the child grows older. The variety of styles of interaction include:

Influence Interaction Styles

Mom-Driven	Child-Driven
Providing	Requesting
Choice-Offering	Reacting
Asking	

Mom-Driven

Providing is defined here as mom offering products without explicit communication from the child. She may very well be considering the wants and needs of her child at the same time she considers her own set of values, or she may operate mostly on the basis of what she considers best. Quoting the mother of a boy aged 3 from the 2005 *WonderGroup Mom/Kid Influence Study*:

> I buy things that my 3-year-old *will like*, but also make sure that it's healthy or appropriate for his age.

This quote suggests that mom is making purchase decisions by projecting what her child will like without the explicit communication from the child. So even when mom is operating on her own values, she is always considering the child to some extent.

Choice-Offering is the next style we have observed. This is when mom explicitly offers alternatives and asks for the child's input. Go to any store and you will see moms offering their children choices, often saying something like, "Would you like this one or this one?" With this style she is still maintaining a high level of control over what can be chosen, but she is purposefully engaging her child in the process. Why does she do this? I remember watching a mom and her son during a shop-along study of kids' clothing stores. She led her son through the store picking out items she thought were good, all the while talking about some of the features and pros and cons of the items she was choosing, and repeatedly asking him which item he would like. When I questioned her later about her style, she explained that she believed that this was a way to teach her son how to make decisions. Other moms we have talked to suggest that this approach also builds some "buy-in" on the part of their children, ensuring that they will use the product once they get it home. Another version of choice-offering is when mom chooses the occasion and particular brand, but allows the child to choose the flavor or variety.

Asking is the final mom-driven style we have seen. It is a common occurrence every evening for moms to ask their children, "What do you want for dinner?" Of course, asking occurs in all kinds of situations, as mom simply wants to short circuit the discussion and go straight to the source, her kid. In most cases, she is genuinely seeking information and help regarding choices for her child. She still holds some control over the decision, maintaining the right to veto the child's choice if she should deem it inappropriate. As kids get to be tweens and teens, mom even views the child as having more expertise regarding certain subjects or products than she does.

We know, however, that moms are not all alike when it comes to how they behave towards their children. We performed a segmentation analysis of moms in the 2004 Simmons study. We identified a continuum of parenting styles from more permissive to more restrictive. The overall proportion is 40/60 permissive versus restrictive. While the influence interaction styles we've discussed are present for all moms, the frequency and application of these styles is dependent on where a mom falls on the continuum. Permissive moms are more likely to use the kid-empowering styles of asking and choice-offering, and be more responsive to kid requests. The Restrictive moms favor the more mom-control styles of providing and choice-offering.

Child-Driven

From a kid-driven perspective, there are two modes of interaction—requesting and reacting.

Request is when the child explicitly makes her wants known to mom through any sort of communication. There is, of course, the universally understood, "I want that," kind of request, but, especially with younger children, requests are often more subtle, such as pointing or picking up a product. Younger children, under age 6, are more likely to use this type of request because their verbal skills are not as well developed as those of older children.

Reaction is the final, and perhaps most powerful, kid-driven interaction style. It is clear that even when mom is using either the providing or choice-offering style, the child's reaction to her offering is paramount. It is an immutable truth that if a child does not like a product intended for her own use or consumption, then the child will not use it or consume it. To validate this truth, simply observe a parent who attempts to serve baby food peas to an infant or toddler who, for reasons unknown, does not like peas. Those peas usually end up on the face of the parent. And, since few parents are willing to endure "peas in the face" more than a few times (the first time seems kind of funny), there is a second immutable truth of kid reaction which is that *mom will not buy what the child will not use or consume*. Thus, a child's "veto power" is always in play no matter what the product is.

The flip-side of a child's negative reaction or veto is when mom observes that her child has a positive reaction to a product or service. In this case, she will likely store that information as a guide to future purchases. This phenomena explains why kids do not need to continuously request the same things, as mom will move forward and buy previously requested items based on a positive experience by her and the child.

Child Reaction is also the primary way in which children end up influencing a wide variety of purchase decisions that do not involve them directly. The communication might go something like this, "You're not going to buy that car are you Dad; it's for grandpas!" Okay, so maybe another car instead. This type of unsolicited opinion-offering is particularly prevalent among tweens and teens, who seem to have an opinion about everything and also seem to know it all.

With the various mutual decision-making styles in mind, we can now frame the life stages of the 4i4l consumer in a way that goes beyond just age of child. The stages are shown on a continuum by age of child, as follows:

Dependence	Conditional	Interdependence
0 1 2	*3 4 5 6 7 8*	*9 10 11 12*

Dependence Stage

The *Dependence* stage begins in pregnancy and spans through infancy into the terrible two's, ending just before pre-school. The dependence stage, as the title implies, is a period when mom is making almost all decisions on behalf of the child, with little or no direct feedback from the child. This is not to say that the child does not influence mom's decisions, as the child's influence begins even in the womb. Rather, it is a stage when mom makes decisions based on her own needs, and on her inference of the needs of her child and *provides* products and brands to her child. As the child approaches the age of 2 years mom will begin *Choice-Offering* and some *Asking* her child for preferences. In quantitative terms, the dependence stage is as follows:

Influence Interaction Styles: Dependence Stage

Mom-Driven		Child-Driven	
Providing	High	Requesting	Very Low
Choice-Offering	Low	Reacting	Low
Asking	Very Low		

Mom versus Child Balance: 90/10

Pregnancy

Perhaps you are surprised that pregnancy is a consideration of the 4i4l, as the child is not even born. You may be wondering how mother and child act as one 4i4l consumer when the child has no voice, no presence, and no preferences. But, if you think about it, this is where the 4i4l consumer really begins. Every expectant mom is filled with dreams, aspirations, expectations, and anxieties about what it will be like to be a mom. Will she be a good mom? How will she know what to do? Will her child be healthy? Will her child achieve great things? Will her child have a life that is better than her own? A moms ruminates over these and many more questions prior to her child's birth. This is where a child's influence comes into play— influence that drives hundreds of millions of dollars of consumption, all in anticipation of the big event.

Every expectant couple can recount their very first encounters with their not-yet-born child. This typically begins with the very first baby video, the ultra-sound. There she is, heart beating, sometimes swimming around, right on the video monitor. The bonding begins. Eventually, mom will actually feel her child move inside. It seems random at first, but moms report that their children seem to *react* to some of things they eat. Something a bit too spicy, or a little caffeine, and the child is letting mom know they are not too happy with a swift kick in the ribs. If

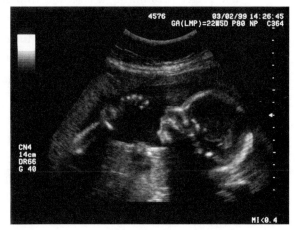

mom figures out what she did to cause the issue, then there is also teaching-learning that modifies future behaviors. And while mother and child are physically connected via the umbilical cord, they are undeniably individuals.

Of course the main type of mutual decision-making that is exhibited during pregnancy is *providing* as mom anticipates the arrival of the child and seeks to satisfy both hers and the child's needs in advance. In fact, pregnancy may be the most powerful driver of behavior change and consumption that exists. Virtually overnight, most expectant moms modify their lifestyles as a result of pregnancy. Coffee drinkers give up the daily Starbucks. Smokers stop smoking. Junk food eaters begin to eat their vegetables and brain food. And almost all begin to take a daily prenatal vitamin that is too big to swallow, and often causes them to be nauseated. Additionally, a significant amount of consumption can be traced to pregnancy.

One of our clients is Evenflo Baby Products. They make and market a complete line of baby care products, ranging from bottles to car seats, to strollers, and just about everything else in-between. It is our job to understand the ever-evolving new class of first-time moms. Their preferences and approach to impending motherhood tells us a lot about what kind of moms they will be. We know that most moms seek information about baby care products and form their initial brand preferences during the second trimester of pregnancy, with the bulk of purchases made during the third trimester. We've even referred to this as the "120-Day War" as the fortunes of a baby-care brand such as Evenflo are won or lost every 120-days as a new group of first time moms move into their second and third trimesters, and the current group moves on.

During this 120-day period these moms are highly attuned to information about baby care and baby-care products. They seek out recommendations from trusted friends, their own mothers, and their obstetricians or gynecologists. They search the web for information that is credible and useful, and they develop an extensive shopping list for themselves and for friends and relatives. We also know that many first-time parents now begin the consideration of some big-ticket items such as a new car to replace that sporty two-seater, and even a new house with room for baby, located in an area with good schools. They may also begin to think about life insurance and a will for the first time in their lives. Imagine, all of this behavior and purchasing being driven by a person that is not yet born. Now that's influence.

From a marketing point of view, it is important to know that few first-time moms-to-be enter into motherhood with a high level of self-confidence regarding this monumental role. Even the most self-assured professionals may feel terrified at their incompetence with this new position in life. As such, they desire brands that offer strong reassurance that they are making a smart decision for their baby.

Infancy

Infancy begins with the cutting of the umbilical cord that has physically connected mother and child for nine months. However, it could be argued that just as someone whose arm has been amputated can still feel the missing arm, so do moms still remain invisibly connected to their child. Now that mom has a living, breathing, crying, nursing, burping, pooping, and occasionally sleeping infant to take care of, her world is hyper-focused on the needs of her child. In a sense, the physical connection of pregnancy is replaced by a connection of dependency. The child cannot survive without the physical and emotional care of its mother or at least another human being.

The momentous bond between mother and child plays a significant role in the development and health of the child starting from the day of birth. Human contact and emotional care are imperative to the healthy maturation of a child. James Prescott, Ph.D. suggests, "During formative periods of brain growth certain types of sensory deprivation such as lack of touching and rocking by the mother result in incomplete or damaged development of the neuronal systems that control affection." In other words, when the instinctive behaviors of infants such as sucking, grasping, and crying are neglected and or not reinforced by the mother, the child can become severely socially impaired and further can develop several acute health problems. Furthermore, there have been numerous studies conducted on the intriguing topic of infants and human contact.

During the 1930s Renne Splitz followed by John Bowlby studied infant deaths in foundling homes and in long-term hospitalization. These sterile environments lacked visual and tactile stimulation and although they had adequate care in the strict sense, human contact was notably absent. A significant percentage of these babies died in the first year. Following this study, Harry Harlow experimented with social isolation in newborn monkeys, which extended from birth to as long as one year. The study showed that these monkeys were severely socially impaired, at times apathetic, hyperactive, and had occasional outbursts of violence.

These studies show that there is an undeniable force of nature that binds mother and baby across all walks of life. It is obvious that mother and child work as a team, in an interdependent relationship necessary for survival. The psychiatrist D. W. Winnicott declares, "There was never just an infant, but an infant-mother pair."

While the need for physical care and feeding is obvious, the infant's need for emotional connection is interesting in that it underscores the power of the relationship between mother and child. The nature of 4i4l relationship during infancy is intense in both directions of providing-reacting, as mom and child engage in a crash course of learning. There is an old maxim that "the baby needs a blanket when mom is cold." This is an example of the *Providing* style, as mom uses her own senses to determine the needs of her child. But, infancy is a period of high feedback between mom and child that creates the foundation of conditioning for future 4i4l influence.

So what does this feedback look like? As the table below highlights, all of the communication from the infant is non-verbal and, interestingly, so too is mom's.

Child's Need State	Child's Behavior	Mom's Response
Hungry	Rooting/Crying	Feeds
Playful	Quiet/Smiles/Laugh	Smiles/Laughs
Anxious/Uncomfortable	Frown/Crying	Investigates
Sleepy	Crankiness/Crying	Sings/Rocks
Curious	Reaches/Stares	Offers Item

The pattern of behaviors illustrated above show very clearly how moms are conditioned early on to respond to the needs of their child. In the case of an infant, these needs are all expressed without language, so moms learn the "language" of their infants which is subtle yet effective. Moms report that they eventually learn what different types of crying indicate. It is probably true for most infants that 100 percent of their requests are granted, as their moms anxiously await any communication from their children.

It is interesting and informative to examine the marketing approach of Procter and Gamble in the diaper category. They have two brands, Pampers and Luvs, which are positioned to address the needs of first-time and experienced moms, respectively. Pampers is the premium brand that offers all the latest "bells and whistles" while Luvs is offered as a value brand that is more basic in its offering. Pampers appeals to the mom who wants only the best for her child, and seeks the reassurance of a "partner." P&G even offers the Pampers Parenting Institute, which it describes as follows on its website:

> The Pampers Parenting Institute is committed to providing parents with the best in information and support from the world's leading experts in child health and development.

This is music to the ears of a first-time mom who needs the highest assurance of quality and credible support. Luvs, on the other hand, seems to be positioned more toward the experienced mom who, having already survived one baby, can now take a more relaxed approach, one that looks to the experience of other moms, instead of professionals or institutions. So, instead of a Parenting Institute, Luvs offers moms an opportunity to "chat" with other moms on its website.

This is a smart strategy that provides a strong positioning to first-time "point-of-entry" moms with Pampers, knowing that many of these moms will stick with the brand with subsequent children. The strategy also protects the flank of the company against lower priced competitors with Luvs, knowing that experienced moms become more likely to migrate to less expensive options.

Conditional Stage

The next stage of the 4i4l is the *Conditional* stage, which commences when the child is about age two, continuing until about age eight. The defining characteristic of the Conditional stage of the 4i4l is that the child becomes increasingly more verbal and expressive of her wants and needs, yet mom still moderates the dialogue, evaluating every request and, of course, providing for the child based on what she believes is best. In marked contrast to the Dependence stage, moms now increase the level of *Choice-Offering*, using the process of shopping as a developmental opportunity. Also important is that the child begins to directly *Request* versus simply *Reacting* to mom's offerings. Further, the child's verbal abilities allow her to react more specifically and vociferously than before. The mix of styles are as shown below:

Influence Interaction Styles: Conditional Stage

Mom-Driven		Child-Driven	
Providing	Moderate	Requesting	Moderate
Choice-Offering	Moderate	Reacting	High
Asking	Low-Moderate		

Mom versus Child Balance 50/50

From a marketer's point of view, the increase in Choice-Offering, Asking, and Kid Requesting and Reacting during the Conditional stage clearly argues the need for establishing brand recognition and liking among kids. It has been shown in research and in practice that kids of this age (4 to 7) will "choose" or "prefer" brands or products with which they are familiar. Of course, this is also the stage when it is imperative to market to moms, as they are in control of the set of acceptable options that will be offered and are far more likely to refuse the requests of their child than when the child becomes a tween or teen.

Pre-School (Aged 2 to 5)

The need for both mom and kid marketing increases and evolves as the child moves from younger to older. For 2-to-5-year-olds, mom is still in the providing mode, but will be keen on how her child reacts to products. She will also increase choice-offering, both as a way to help "educate" her child on decision-making, and as a way to avoid the inconvenience of her child refusing or reacting negatively to her choice. The pre-school years are marked by the highest concern for development of basic skills, such as language, counting, colors, and even beginner reading. With this focus in mind, brands often can find traction by becoming some part of this developmental process.

A case in point is Johnson & Johnson's Buddies brand of personal care products for pre-schoolers, or 2-to-5-year-olds. From a 4i4l stage perspective, this age group spans from the Dependence Stage across

The Early Conditional Stage suggests that some level of kid involvement and influence are critical. J&J Buddies has a brand-identity that will both appeal to the child and help mom teach healthy hygiene.

to the Early Conditional Stage, suggesting that some level of kid involvement and influence are critical. In helping J&J develop the Buddies brand, we created a brand-identity that would both appeal to the child and help mom teach healthy hygiene. In a sense, the brand becomes a conduit of communication between mother and child. The characters are undeniably appealing to the target age group, and at the same time serve the function of communicating the intended use of the product. We have watched moms turn these characters into a game of teaching their children how to bathe.

Without an intimate knowledge of the 4i4l consumer, this product line might have been developed as only an efficacy or convenience-based platform, addressing the needs of the mom only, with little regard to the child or the interaction between the mother and child. There is no doubt that this approach, so often used by companies, would have been far less successful than the approach which acknowledges the needs of both mom and child, and their interaction. The rich consumer experience expressed by the J&J Buddies brand is in stark contrast to many other initiatives that target this age group, where the manufacturer simply places a licensed character on the label, hoping that it will appeal to mom and child.

The Kid Years (Aged 4 to 7)

If the target for a brand is the older end of the conditional stage, then the need to address the child is critical. One such brand is Kid Cuisine. This brand appeals to kids from age 3 to as old as age 10. The older child begins to request more frequently than the preschooler, and mom begins to ask more—both of which move the balance of influence power towards the child. The driver of this new influence interaction style is that mom wants to help her child develop confidence in decision-making. This priority is perfectly reflected in the advertising for the brand, as shown here in storyboard format.

The 4i4l Influence Interaction Styles that are portrayed are mom asking and kid request. Note the dialogue: Mom says, "You guys look hungry." This is a classic mom *asking* moment. The kids then respond

ConAgra
"Fire Dept"
:30
8/29/2005

KIDS RUN OVER TO KITCHEN ISLAND AND MOM.

MOM: You guys look hungry. Anything sound good?

BOY: I know what I want.
SFX/LFX: Lights and siren.

KIDS TURN AND LOOK TOWARD FRONT DOOR.

SFX/LFX: Continues.

SFX: Crash!
KC: Cheese blaster comin' thru!
BOY: Kid Cuisine!
GIRL: Just in time!

KC IS TOSSED AROUND BY THE WILD FIRE HOSE.

KC: Whoo-hoo!
SFX: Sirens and lights.

THE PRODUCT FLOATS ON A GEYSER OF CHEESE.

KC: My Kid Cuisine Cheese Blaster Mac and Cheese Meal is non-stop fun!

BOY: With lots of gooey cheese!

GIRL: To blast how you please!

CAMERA PULLS OUT AS KC SPINS THE FIRE HOSE REEL.

KC: Let's roll out the fun with my berry-flavored fruit roll.
BOY: Berry delicious!

KC AND THE KIDS TURN TO LOOK AT THE GROWING AND BULGING HOSE BEHIND THEM.

MOM: Having fun?
KC: Actually, we're having (pause) ... a blast!

CUT TO A CLOSE UP OF THE TIED OFF HOSE ... STRETCHING AND THEN BURSTING IN AN EXPLOSION OF CHEESE.

SFX: BAM!!!!!!

KC ENTERS FRAME.

KC: Mealtime is funtime with Kid Cuisine!

The 4i4l Influence Interaction Styles portrayed in this Kid Cuisine ad are Mom Asking and Kid Request.

to the dramatic entry of the brand character, Kid Cuisine, with a *request* response, "Kid Cuisine!" We've found that dramatizing the 4i4l Influence Interaction Style in advertising helps to drive actual activation of consumer behavior. This goes beyond the typical advertising approaches that simply focus on brand awareness and image.

Interdependence Stage

The *Interdependence* stage correlates with the tween and young teen segment of children aged 8 to 14. This is the stage when anything that is used directly by the child must be marketed directly to the child. The reasons for this are two-fold. First, the attitudes of kids in this age group move from "mom knows what I like" to "mom doesn't really know what I like." Moms are slow to catch on to this fact, until they realize that many of the products they are buying for their child are going unused, and, in some cases, are mysteriously lost. The kids are loath to admit that mom doesn't get it anymore, as one girl sheepishly admitted in a focus group, "I won't tell my mom I don't like the clothes she buys for me because I don't want to hurt her feelings." Secondly, moms are far more trusting child of this age to make requests that are sensible, so the frequency of mom vetoes are far less than with younger children. The dynamics of Mom and Kid Influence Interaction Styles are as follows:

Influence Interaction Styles: Interdependence Stage

Mom-Driven		Child-Driven	
Providing	Low-Moderate	Requesting	Moderate-High
Choice-Offering	Moderate	Reacting	Moderate
Asking	High		

Mom versus Child Balance   25/75

This stage is called the Interdependence stage because moms begin to rely on their child to help guide them in purchase decisions, certainly for the children, but also increasingly for other family purchases. The 2005 *WonderGroup Mom/Kid Influence Study* showed that a mom of tweens and young teens was much more likely to say that her child influenced the purchase decisions for all-family products, and even such products as her own clothing.

An interesting example of marketing to this stage is a spot we created for Hasbro's ChatNow Communicators. As background, the ChatNow product uses advanced two-way radio technology to deliver some of the functionality of a cell phone. It looks like a cell phone, and in many ways acts like a cell phone, except that it requires no monthly fees or usage charges. The one thing this age group desires most is a cell phone, even more than an iPod. Further, while actual cell phone ownership among tweens and young teens is growing fast, most moms are strongly resistant to the idea of their children racking up monster bills chatting away at cell phone rates. Thus, our advertising strategy was to prepare tweens with the knowledge they would need to overcome potential objections that mom would raise. We did this by dramatically showing mom refusing to allow her children a cell-phone and comes to understand that ChatNow is a two-way communicator with a 2-mile radius. Thus, the talk time is free.

This is an example of "scripting" for the tween who is now expected by mom to provide a sound rationale for purchase requests. The implication is that marketers should consider what the child will say to his parent, and how it will likely be received. I am reminded of the PlayStation 2 launch that cleverly included a DVD player that kids were able to pitch as a great value-added feature to their parents, many of whom at that time were considering the purchase of a DVD player. It is actually somewhat gratifying to moms when their children come prepared with a sound, well-thought-out argument, as it demonstrates that the child is becoming a smart consumer.

In summary, the 4i4l consumer evolves through three stages: Dependence, Conditional, and Interdependence. These stages represent the different Influence Interaction Styles between mom and child. For mom, these are Providing, Choice-offering, and Asking. For the child, they are Requesting and Reacting. The nature of each stage pro-

Hasbro
Ninja Mom
:30
8/29/2005

A SALESMAN JUMPS FROM A TREE, LAND-ING IN FRONT OF MOM AND KIDS.
SFX: GONG AND THUD.

SALESMAN HOLDS UP A CHATNOW.
SFX: PHONE RINGS
SALESMAN: Hey kids, want one?

THE KIDS ARE EXCITED. MOM IS IRRITATED.
KIDS: Cool! A cell phone!

MOM FLIPS OVER TOP OF KIDS LIKE IN A KUNG FU MOVIE.
MOM: You may not...

IN A NINJA-LIKE MANNER, MOM BLOCKS ATTEMPTS TO HAND PHONE TO KIDS.
MOM: ...have a cell phone.

THE SALESMAN CONTINUES HIS ATTEMPTS.
SFX: TWIRLING WIND AND BOINKS.
SALESMAN: Step off, ninja mom. It's not a cell phone.

MOM MAKES KUNG FU FACE.
SFX: NECK CRACK.
MOM: Eeewwwww.

SALESMAN COUNTERS WITH A CHATNOW IN EACH HAND.
SALESMAN: The ChatNow communicator is a new way for kids to talk, text message...

MOM GOES FROM ANGRY TO SWEET AS MAN SNAPS HER PICTURE.
SFX: CLICK.
SALESMAN: ...and take pictures.

SALESMAN HOLDS UP CHATNOWS.
SALESMAN: And if you buy a pair, staying in touch is totally free.

KIDS: Free!

MOM PLAYFULLY HOLDS FOOT UP TO SALESMAN'S CHEEK.
MOM: Really free?
SALESMAN: Really free.

KIDS HOLD PHONES UP TO SCREEN. LOGO AND URL SUPER.
SFX: WHOOSH.
ANNCR: ChatNow 2-way communicator.
Batteries not included. Zero-to-two-mile range will vary.

ChatNow's advertising prepares tweens with the knowledge needed to overcome potential objections their moms will raise.

vides insights into how to effectively market to moms and kids in these stages. In total, this view of the decision-making process between mom and child suggests a far more collaborative process than the traditional gatekeeper mom versus nagging-child model that has been in vogue for many years.

4

Mom and Kid Motivators, or Getting to Win-Win

IN CHAPTER 3, we introduced the concept of how moms and kids function as a team, referring to this partnership as the Four-Eyed-Four-Legged (4i4l) consumer and discussed how the relationship begins before birth and evolves over time. Our focus in that discussion was on the nature of the relationship between mom and child from the standpoint of how each of them influences the other. We referred to this as the styles of influence interaction. In Chapter 4 we will build on this understanding of the 4i4l by revealing a model of the motivators for the 4i4l. Whereas Chapter 3 discussed the "what," this chapter will help to answer the "why." Why is it that mom provides, offers choices, or simply asks her child what he wants? And, why does a kid request certain products or react the way she does? The answers are found in understanding what motivates both moms and kids.

The one big truth here is that brands that are successful with this consumer segment address the motivators of *both* mom and kid. There is no enduring brand that exists as a win-lose proposition in the mind of the 4i4l consumer. To believe otherwise ultimately leads marketers to adopt wrong-headed approaches, such as "nag-factor" marketing from a kid-driven perspective or to believe that they are marketing a "mom-only" brand. Both of these approaches are in reality win-lose propositions. The "nag factor" mentality believes that you can be successful by creating such strong appeal to the kid that she will overwhelm mom with nagging requests, even if the product offers nothing for the mom. This is a win for the child and a loss for mom. The "mom-only" version of this believes that you can be successful by offering such a strong appeal to mom, that she will force her child to consume or use the product. This is a win for mom, but a loss for the child.

How is it, you ask, that brand managers and their management constantly fall into the win-lose traps discussed above? We believe that it is because they confuse brand strategy with marketing execution. Instead of clearly defining how a brand delivers against both of its constituents, they focus only on the question of advertising and media mix. Should we advertise to moms or should we advertise to kids, or both? While this is certainly an important consideration, it is secondary to the job of defining how the brand will deliver against the needs of both moms and kids. Once this is understood, then the question of marketing mix can be addressed.

To help illuminate the needs of both moms and kids we developed a model of Mom and Kid Motivators that highlights the major motivational themes that are in play for brands that are used by kids. The Mom and Kid Motivators model has three main components: Mom Motivators, Kid Motivators, and the Influence Interaction Styles. This model was developed based on our collective experience across a wide range of categories, and by examining the marketing efforts of many

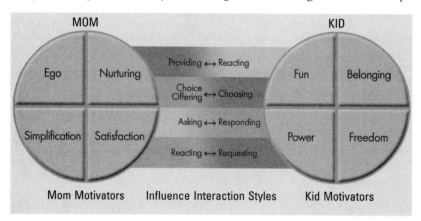

brands that have the 4i4l consumer as their customer. We will describe each component of the model, and then discuss a successful case that will bring the model to life.

This model guides nearly everything we do at our WonderGroup Advertising and our LaunchForce New Product Development agencies. Our advertising is stronger and deeply persuasive because it is explicitly informed by motivational strategy. Our new product and brand development is more successful because we are able to use the motivational platforms to deliberately explore new opportunities. Frankly, this is our "secret sauce."

Mom Motivators

There are four major motivators for moms as they make decisions regarding kid/family products: Ego, Simplification, Nurturing, and Satisfaction. Each of these basic motivators relates to and helps identify consumer insights.

Ego. This represents a mom's need for a positive self-image. Some of the specific articulations of insights that come from this motive are:

Good mom: Moms want to be perceived as being a good parent, doing the "right" thing. The culture defines the role of motherhood, and moms are often motivated to live up to it.

Family affirmation: It is just human nature to want the affirmation and appreciation of others and moms are no exception, wanting their kids and or spouse to appreciate what they do.

Smart mom: The need to feel that they are making a good or smart decision is a strong desire among moms. They may express this as, "I like when I have figured something out that others may not have or when I have information that can help others."

Sneaky mom: A version of the smart mom driver is when moms feel like they have provided something good for their kids, but the kids didn't even know it. This is where the "you know it's nutritious, they know it's delicious" idea comes from.

Prestige: Although they might not admit it openly, "it feels good to own certain products that are more exclusive or elite" is a sentiment that often motivates a mom's behavior.

Simplification. In our modern society, the need for simplification and convenience is unending. Some examples:

Time saving: We've often heard moms say, "I am always looking for ways to save time with chores so I have time for more important things like spending quality time with my family." The notion of saving time for more important things is one of the key values of today's GenX mom. The Baby Boomer mom might have been more likely to express saving time as a means to accomplishing more.

Ease: There are a number of ways in which this motive is expressed. The first is to make it easier to do something that is valued, such as preparing a fine meal. There is also the proposition of making certain interactions easier, as in, "When I know what my kids want, it makes my life easier."

Reduction of physical labor or unpleasantness: Drudgery, which is constantly being redefined, is forever a point of opportunity. By understanding each and every moment of unpleasantness in the consumer experience, we can uncover new ways to delight moms.

Elimination of family conflict: There are certain situations that seem to cause conflict between family members. Moms state that they wish there was a way to reduce or eliminate conflict, saying, "I don't want to have to fight to get my kids to use/consume something I buy."

Efficacy/Durability: "I don't have time for things that don't work or break down" is the way moms view products today. Many will pay for high quality.

Trust/Confidence: Trust in brands and advertising is at an all-time low, so brands that can garner today's moms' trust are rare and powerful. She wants to be able to trust brands when she doesn't have all the information or expertise, or when the risk of a wrong decision is costly.

Reduction of choices or indecision: Today's marketplace is overflowing with choices, so sometimes moms just need someone or something to simplify the decisions, to be a partner in the process.

Nurturing. A mom's need to nurture begins early, arguably when she was a child. Insights that are related to nurturing are as follows:

Child development—mental and physical: More than ever before, Moms are acutely tuned into the objective of helping their children progress both mentally and physically.

Safety/well-being: The world we live in today has created a stronger focus by moms on protecting their children from harm.

Sustenance/good for health of child: Moms want to be sure that their children are getting the nutrition they need to grow and be healthy.

Provides child self-esteem/confidence: One of the emerging values of today's moms is the desire to cultivate their children's confidence, self-esteem, and future success.

Satisfaction. Arguably, the most powerful motive for moms is to make their children happy. There are two insight areas that exist here, as follows:

Child enjoyment: Talk to any mom and you'll hear, "Nothing makes me happier than to see a smile on my child's face." Of course this is a natural and normal expression of a parent's love for her child, and is typically offered with appropriate parent responsibility. We've identified a more permissive mom segment that seems to respond to this motive more than others based on an underlying value of wanting to provide more to their children than they had as a child.

Child popularity: Every mom remembers the trials and tribulations of fitting in as a child, which makes them sensitive to whether their children fit in. We've often heard "I don't want them to be left out or teased."

Kid Motivators

Just as there are four major motivational areas for moms, we have found four major areas for kids, which are: Fun, Power, Belonging, and Freedom. In our last book, *The Great Tween Buying Machine,* we explained these areas and broke them down into a number of different centrics. Here, we simplify and modify these somewhat for the 4i4l consumer model.

Fun. It has been said many times that the work of kids is to have fun, and of course this is true. Nearly any kid product includes a healthy helping of fun. Truth is, though, to be an enduring brand, marketers must deliver more than just fun. Breaking it down from a motivational perspective, we look at fun as follows:

Sensation: Kids enjoy pleasurable sensory experiences, such as bright colors, scents, sour tastes, or a rush of excitement or thrill. The desire for sensory experience grows and evolves as kids grow into tweens and teens. One of the most interesting examples of this motive is the popularity of strongly fragranced shampoos and cleaning products that most certainly appeal to tweens and teens.

Interactivity: They will twist and turn, and stretch and stir, dip and dunk, deriving enjoyment from the action alone. Many adults cannot understand the appeal of a product such as Lunchables Pizza that kids eat with cold bread, cold sauce, and cold cheese. This is not a great pizza experience, but it offers the opportunity to build it the way you want it, and this seems to be its own reward.

Amusement: Sometimes kids just want to be silly or laugh. Products that facilitate laughter and silliness can have a place in their hearts.

Satiety: Before lunch or after school, kids' fast revving engines begin to thirst for fuel. They'll say, "I crave something to feed my hunger, satisfy my sweet tooth, re-energize me."

Imagination/creativity: Kids' imaginations are their vehicles, which can transport them to new and exotic places to meet amazing people. Many products are based on providing the portal to this imaginary world, including such perennial favorites as Barbie and GI Joe.

Power. For the most part, kids live in a world where they don't have a lot of power or control over their circumstances, so it is not surprising that brands that offer this can be very motivating. Some of the particular insights around the power motive are:

Control: They say, "I want to be able to have influence on my world. I want my voice to be heard." Brands such as Nickelodeon have done a good job of giving kids the sense of control with such programs as the Kids' Choice Awards. Others build in elements of customization into their products.

Mastery: Kids are driven to master new skills, especially as they grow into the tween years. This desire is reinforced in school from early on. We've heard them offer, "I feel good when I have mastered a game or achieved a goal." This is one of the key drivers behind video games.

Belonging. As discussed earlier, the need for belonging begins very early, with young children needing a physical and emotional connection to their parents. As they grow into tweens and beyond, the need for belonging to parents is replaced by a similar need to belong to their group of peers.

Nurturing: There is an interesting recent example of products whose appeal is largely based on the desire of the child to nurture, such as Neopets. This website offers kids and tweens the ability to adopt and care for virtual fantasy pets and characters. Of course, a little girl's first baby doll has always filled this need.

Popularity: Kids want to be accepted by friends. The desire to "fit-in" is strong, especially among tweens. The notion of prestige is also related to this motive. Certain brands can be said to have "badge value" which is simply saying that the user will gain some social currency or prestige just by using or owning such a brand.

Identity: Closely related to popularity, kids, tweens, and teens seek to establish their identity. This can be in the form of affinity with an activity, such as sports, or other established and recognized entities. Sometimes it is with a peer group. We've seen many tweens who claim their fashion as expressing their identity, which happens to be almost precisely the same as their friends.

Freedom. The desire for freedom shows itself in different ways as kids grow from young children into tweens and, finally into independent teens. The constellation of insights related to the freedom motive are as follows:

Exploration: Young children learn through exploration of their environment, touching, tasting, and manipulating anything that happens to capture their attention. You can probably describe what licking the floor would taste like. Why do you think that is? Exploration never really ceases, but rather it expands to more adventurous and even dangerous places as kids grow into teens. Successful brands leveraging this motive find ways to offer safe exploration that is appropriate to the age of the child.

Empowerment: Young kids want to get bigger. Tweens want to do what teens do. Teens want to live on their own away from their parents. Brands and products can be based on delivering the empowerment to independence. A case in point is Kraft's Easy Mac that is designed to allow tweens the ability to make their own afternoon snack.

The Lunchables Story

Now that we have delved into the various dimensions of motivation for both moms and kids, we illustrate how brands can put it all together to get to win-win propositions. Our case is Lunchables from Oscar Mayer. If you are not familiar with this brand, it is a lunch kit that offers kids some of their favorite foods in a handy tray, and includes a main entrée, drink, and dessert. For kids, the brand delivers on multi-

A lunch you can both look forward to.

Introducing Lunchables® Chicken Shake-Ups. Made with White Meat Chicken so you can love their lunch as much as they do. Now that's reason to smile and let them shake away. **Lunchables!** Pack a Smile.™

ple motivators: the fun/sensory enjoyment of food they like, the fun/interactivity of building your own food, and the belonging/popularity of a brand that has "badge value" in the lunch room.

The brand has always been intensely popular with kids under the age of ten, but the same cannot be said for moms. Many moms would describe the brand as too expensive, not very healthy, and not very appetizing. Despite this, the brand has sales approaching $1 billion annually. Why is this? Well, the brand has worked hard to achieve win-win by providing moms with a positioning that says roughly, "your kid works hard at school, doesn't he deserve a treat like Lunchables, that you know will make him happy?" They go on to say "your kid will love you for it."

The first is an example of the satisfaction/child enjoyment motive, with the second well representing ego/family affirmation. By re-framing the issue from one of price-value and nutrition to one of a well-deserved treat, moms are able to rationalize the product and take advantage of its convenience without guilt (simplification). So, as is clear from this case, even brands that appear to be driven by kid appeal can have equally strong mom motives at work.

5

The Decision-Making Process of 4i4l

SOME OF THE MOST prevalent questions we receive as consultants are: "Do I advertise to the moms or to the kids or to both?" "Should my package or location appeal to moms, kids, or both?" "Does my product have to appeal to moms or to kids?" "Who do I do research against?" Frankly, a lot of this depends on how the 4i4l consumer goes about making its purchase and use decision regarding your product or service. But, as you have seen in Chapter 4, we feel that it is safe to say that *both* mom and her kid must be satisfied in some way. Said another way, in the vast majority of situations, kids will *definitely* be a factor.

If we are going to have the greatest chance of positively affecting our consumer's decision toward purchasing our product or service, it only stands to reason that we must first understand how the parent-child interaction affects how the consumer goes about making her decision in the first place.

To begin to answer this puzzle, you should try to understand certain keys involving mom and her child. As Dr. Langbourne Rust told a conference on marketing to kids: "The first [understanding] is that the best salespersons to sell your product to children is their parents, and the second is that the best persons to sell to parents are their children."

The second key is to realize that while everyone knows that children naturally learn from their parents, smart marketers know that parents also learn—and *like to learn*—from their children. As moms reported in the *Motherhood Study*: "Motherhood is all encompassing, fulfilling, an opportunity for ongoing education. You're constantly learning new things." Even moms of teens report learning about "a whole new world of new things" through their children's interests in music, math, science, and education.

Another key is to realize that from the very earliest ages, children have a natural desire to do things for themselves. For example, just a few weeks ago, one of our wives told us about a friend of hers who visited an out-of-town zoo with her 3-year-old granddaughter. When she asked her friend what she thought of the zoo, her friend replied:

> I have no idea. I never got to see it. When we got to the zoo, my granddaughter had to use the bathroom. So, we went in, did our thing, and then I washed her hands. As soon as we left the restroom she started to scream! She cried and screamed and pouted and wouldn't stop. No matter where I tried to take her, she kept up the crying, pouting, screaming scene until finally, after only 30 minutes at the zoo, I had it! I dragged her back to the car and we left.
>
> As soon as we pulled out of the parking lot, she fell asleep. After she took her little nap, she woke up much calmer and I asked her, 'What was all of that crying about at the zoo?' You know what she said?
>
> *"It was because I wanted to pump the soap myself!"*

In summary, what ultimately affects the purchase decision is how the child who wants to do things for himself, or at least have a say in all things important to him, and how the mom, who wants to teach, nurture, protect and simplify her life relate to each other.

As you can imagine, we've observed many different ways in which the 4i4l approaches decision making. It will vary depending upon the type of purchase (planned versus impulse), the type of parent (permissive versus restrictive), the price, and the category.

Child's Influence on Mom

In almost every case, it is surprising to see just how important the kid part of our 4i4l is to the ultimate purchasing decision. As we stated earlier, since today's mom seeks to partner with her child for many purchase decisions, the power behind the child part of our 4i4l consumer lies largely in the *influence* they have on mom. research confirms that when it comes to purchasing products or services for their children, only a minority of moms (less than 40 percent) agrees that advertising helps them to make their decision—rather it is the child that helps them do this.

For further perspective, we conducted a quantitative study of 700 moms in May 2005, where we tried to get an even closer look at the power of the child's request versus other factors when it came to purchasing food for their kids. Here, too, we saw evidence of just how big a factor a child request is. Specifically, other than "price," which was statistically even with "child request," no other factor came close.

Especially important is the finding that "child request" is almost three times more important to a mom's purchase decision than advertising she saw herself!

And, interestingly, "child request" in this particular category is so strong that there was no significant difference between Permissive and Restrictive moms.

When buying food for your children, which of the following influences your choice?	
Price	*84%*
Child Request	*83*
Coupons	*49*
Brand Name	*38*
Ads you saw or heard	*31*

SOURCE: *WonderGroup Influence Study*, May 2005.

Considering the above, food marketers of kid food products may want to seriously question why they would advertise to moms instead of to children.

As we have seen in Chapter 3, considering kid influence, the primary 4i4l connection occurs between moms and their children from birth through about the upper tween years (about age 12 to 14). Once a child begins to enter the teen years, her drive for independence actually begins to distance her from her parents in terms of some everyday influence and partnership and, thus, the 4i4l connection, while certainly still there, is usually somewhat weaker as far as every day purchases are concerned.

We caution many of our clients who have come to us wanting to develop or position a family type of food or snack for, or to, teenagers. Teenagers generally have sufficient funds to purchase various snack items on their own without a mom partnership, and in the case of influence, they generally don't care enough about day-to-day food items to invest a lot of effort in an influential discussion. They'd rather save these "influence" investments for higher-priced items like clothing, electronics or, better yet, cars or money.

Today's youth have not only a strong influence on purchases made *for them* by their moms *but also* are strong influencers *on purchases made for mom and the household.*

Don Montouri of *Packaged Facts* reports: "Tweens aren't just making decisions about their own money; they're influencing how those around them spend as well. Households with tweens have entirely different consumer habits. They look for new stores to shop in and take more time to browse while they are shopping."

We have seen children strongly influence such purchases as the *family vacation.* In fact, in our recently completed *Influence Study,* the child reportedly influenced 49 percent of family vacations. Many times it is because the child either asked to go to a certain destination spot, or when asked by the parent, he or she vetoed a desired family vacation spot. The result? Mom and family end up at a specific *child-desired* location.

In our work with the Cincinnati Zoo, we found that in almost every visit by a mom, a child was present. Do you think that mom would have come to the zoo and spent money on herself, if it weren't for the child? In fact we know they would not because the vast majority of those adults who no longer visit the zoo state that it is because their *children* have grown up!

We have seen children influence their moms on what *vehicle* to purchase for the family. Here, our *Influence Study* found that children were influential in more than one-third of all recently purchased automobiles by families with kids aged 2 to 14. Adults often tell us that they found themselves swayed to purchase one type of van over another because their kids found one van would be cool to be seen being picked up in.

Kudos to those automobile manufacturers who have added all those great cup holders and compartments and even video screens that today's kids ask for in cars. Kudos also to such brands as Hummer, for realizing the overwhelmingly strong desire of mom to please her child even in the type of car he arrives in for school!

We have even seen children influence their moms to move or to buy a certain *house*. Let's remember, a primary reason that most young families buy a home to begin with is that they need more rooms for their children. As soon as a prospective family walks into a potential new family home, what does the child do? More times than not, he'll immediately ask to see "his" room. When he sees it, if it looks like a lot of fun —maybe even has a bunk bed—then the pressure is on!

And how many moms buy *themselves* a certain hair cut, a certain blouse, a certain piece of clothing, because her child influenced her to? More than you think as you will see later.

Kid Influence on Kid Products

To get a current look at what the 4i4l consumer has meant to children's influence on many of today's household purchases, we conducted a study in July 2005, asking 800 moms to tell us how much recent purchases for their children were impacted by their children's influence. Here are some of the things we saw.

Kid influence on products purchased for kids	
Percent of moms who said kid influenced the purchase of the item	
Athletic shoes	86%
Kids cleansing product	61
Candy or gum	80
Cold cereal	82
Kids clothing	85
Cookies	76
Fast food restaurant	83
Frozen breakfast	82
Frozen dinner	86
Frozen pizza	70
Fruit snacks	81
Granola bars	86
Kid furniture	64
Kid room décor	79
Computer for child	60
Juices/Juice drinks	81
Movies on VHS or DVD	92
Recorded music	92
Video games	88
Vitamins	53
Yogurt	87

SOURCE: *WonderGroup Influence Study,* July 2005.

HUMMER

Mom: First day. Nervous?
(silence)
Mom: Want me to drop you off here so you can walk up?
Kid: No, you can pull right up.

Mom: You sure you're gonna' be alright?

Kid: Should be.
Mom: Bye honey

KID APPROACHES SCHOOL.

Boy to group of school kids: 'Sup?

School kid: Nice ride.

Hummer realizes mom's strong desire to please her child even in the type of car he arrives in for school.

When it comes to purchasing items *for the child* there is little surprise that the child part of our 4i4l consumer is very much in existence. Basically, mom does not buy without her child influencing her decision. Again, she does not need the aggravation of taking the time or money to buy something her child will not want to use. As some moms stated in our 2005 *WonderGroup Mom/Kid Influence Study*:

> My child's influence on products I buy for them is very important. I would waste a lot of money if they didn't like the products.
>
> MOM OF BOY AGED 5 TO 7

> If the purchase will directly impact him, and only him, much influence will be given.
>
> MOM OF BOY AGED 8 TO 11

While the purchase of kid food items are naturally influenced greatly by the child, it is interesting to note that purchases of furniture, room décor, and computers for the child also are done with his or her input.

Further, as shown below, while kids of all ages seem to be highly influential in the purchases of most items bought for them, older kids (tweens aged 8 to 14) weigh in especially heavily in the purchase of athletic shoes, cleansing products, clothing, frozen breakfasts and furniture—or in other words, mostly non-food areas.

Kid influence on products purchased for kids

Percent of moms who said kid influenced the purchase of the item

Kids aged	2–7	8–11	12–14
Athletic shoes	*76%*	*96%* A	*93%* A
Kids' cleansing products	*52*	*70* A	*76* A
Kids' clothing	*78*	*92* A	*91* A
Frozen breakfasts	*70*	*92* A	*94* A
Kid furniture	*54*	*71* a	*100* AB
Video games	*79*	*88*	*93* A

A=Significant difference at 95% vs K 2-7; B=95% vs K 8-11; a=90% difference vs. K 2-7
SOURCE: 2005 *WonderGroup Mom/Kid influence Study*, July 2005,

Kid Influence on Products Used by Family

To better understand the power of kid influence on more of moms' purchases, we also looked at the influence that a child had when a particular purchase was made not just for him, but reportedly for adults, too.

Kid influence on products used by family

Bar soap	31%	House or apartment	47% *
Bottled water	30	Ice cream	63
Cake mix/icing	48	Internet service provider	24
Candy/gum	64	Juices/Juice drinks	69
Casual restaurants	42	Laundry detergent	25
Cold cereal	75	Movies in theatre	76
Cookies	62	Movies on VHS or DVD	66
Fast food restaurant	68	Pet food	19
Frozen breakfast	64	Recorded music	52
Frozen dinner	49	Carbonated beverages	48
Frozen pizza	55	Salty snacks	55
Fruit snacks	75	Toothpaste	50
Family car	32	Vacation	46
Granola bars	49	Video games	71
Room décor/paint/rug	41	Vitamins	48
Computer for home	29	Yogurt	65

*Drops to 25% among tweens and up

SOURCE: WonderGroup Mom/Kid Influence Study, July 2005.

This is the big AH HA! for most marketers. Again, it should not be surprising to anyone that kids certainly have a big say in products that are purchased *for them* but, thanks to our 4i4l consumer, today's kids are virtually joined at the hip with mom as she makes many of her purchases not just for them, but for the family. Even we were surprised that one in four moms reported that her choice in laundry detergent was impacted by her kids input. How does this happen? Well as one mom of a girl aged 8 to 11 told us:

I buy detergents and soaps that work on them. They also like to choose the scents with me.

And, as we have seen before, as mom's child gets older, he or she is likely to be an even greater part of the purchase decision regarding some of her purchases of products for her family:

Kid influence on products used by family

Kids aged	2–7	8–11	12–14
Candy/gum	53%	72% A	74% A
Casual restaurants	36	46 A	49 A
Cookies	56	66 a	69 A
Frozen pizza	48	58 a	64 A
Granola bars	41	49	65 AB
Movies in theatre	70	80 A	81 A
Recorded music	33	54 A	70 AB
Carbonated beverage	33	58 A	58 A
Salty snacks	47	63 A	64 A
Video games	64	72	84 A

A= Significant difference at 95% vs K 2-7; B 95% vs K 8-11; a=90% difference vs K 2-7
SOURCE: *2005 WonderGroup Mom/Kid Influence Study*, n = 800 moms)

Kid Influence on Products Used by Adults

Last, just for the shock value, we took a look at some purchases mom told us that she made *only for herself and or another adult* and here again we saw the need for mom to please or listen to her child. From her car, to her clothing, to her furniture and household cleaners, her child's input comes into play.

> I ask her all the time if clothes look good on me.
>
> MOM OF GIRL AGED 5 TO 7

Kid influence on products for adults only

Automobiles	40%
Adult cleansing products	20
Adult clothing	20
Adult furniture	23
Room décor	18
Household cleaner	34
Recorded music	21
Carbonated beverage	24

SOURCE: *WonderGroup Influence Study*, July 2005.

The Full Story

The true, awesome power of the kid part of our 4i4l is fully uncovered by looking at the child's influence on *all of mom's purchases* no matter if it was bought just for the child, just for adults or for both. In looking at the chart below, an example would be that kid

influence accounted for 79 percent of *all* fruit snacks brought into the
house.

Kid Influence on products purchased whether for children only, adults only or family

Ranked in order of most influence to least

Fruit snacks	79%	Toothpaste	51%
Video games	77	Cake mix/icing	50
Athletic shoes	77	Recorded music	49
Movies in theaters	77	House/apartment	47
Cold cereals	76	Vitamins	46
Juice drinks	72	Vacation	44
Movies on DVD/VHS	70	Carbonated beverage	43
Fast food restaurants	68	Casual restaurant	41
Frozen breakfasts	66	Room décor	39
Yogurt	65	Automobile	39
Ice cream	64	Bar soap	30
Candy & gum	64	Bottled water	30
Cookies	64	Household cleaners	28
Frozen pizza	56	Laundry detergent	27
Salty snacks	55	Pet food	25
Granola bars	52	Home computer	24
Frozen dinners	51	Internet provider	22

SOURCE: 2005 *WonderGroup Kid/Mom Influence Study.*

Plus, even in those categories where the child part of the 4i4l was
less influential, you must wonder whether it would remain at this
lower level if marketers targeted them directly with a specific product
or service. Importantly, the degree in which the child part of our 4i4l
consumer influences the decision almost always ties closely with familiarity with a brand and this familiarity comes through previous personal experience, peer influence, having observed advertising, or at the
very least having observed something he or she thinks looks familiar
on the package.

Many marketers fail to realize that if a specific category does not
presently exhibit a high degree of child influence, it is possibly because
no item in that category currently markets to youth. Remember that
at one time, categories such as yogurt, vacations, retailers, clothing,

music and many others, had little if any child influence. What's different today? All of these categories now market to children.

For example, in looking at the visitation pattern for our zoo client, we saw that while most of the attendance traced to moms and their children, moms told us, in research, that their children never initiated or asked for the visit. In looking at the zoo's marketing efforts, we saw that it never actually promoted itself directly to the children. Once we initiated a kid-targeted advertising campaign, child requests began to move upwards and so did visitation of the zoo.

So, imagine if a pet food advertised directly to children implying that their pet would love them even more if the child fed them Brand X. Or, think about a brand of bottled water running a kid promotion. Think kid influence in these categories would remain low? Before "Happy Meals," kid influence on fast food dining was probably a fraction of what it is today.

Sometimes we'll find a category that at least some of today's youth have a particular problem being very interested in because, frankly, they have more important needs which they want to influence. For example, teens care less about what specific food moms keep in their freezers as long as it is acceptable to them. Rather, teens are far more desirous of certain clothing, entertainment, cars, and so forth, so not surprisingly, a major increase in recent teen influence occurs in the electronics area. In 2005, for example, it was around the iPod. Teens desire to own the neatest coolest stuff, often costing anywhere from $99 to $499. The problem is that only 10 percent of teens hold a job, and those young workers earn an average of only $29 per week. So guess who is going to be influenced to buy one for their teenagers! Or, if not an iPod, a new cell phone. Three quarters of teens now have one of these and the parents pay for about 75 percent of their wireless plans.

When faced with an obvious mismatch between a product or category and its intended target consumer, you can either try to find the way in which to motivate this target to invest his or her "influence" or, you should look elsewhere for the best target. For example, while a specific snack item may be great for teens, you might want to target the younger tweens in the family in order to get the product into the house, where then, surprise, surprise, the teen will be glad to consume it.

There are many other products and categories we have not looked at in depth, but considering some of the quotes we received from our *Influence Study,* you can be assured that if children touch it in any way, they can be a very important part of our 4i4l decision making process. Here are just some of the quotes to think about from moms of children aged 2 to 14:

> I encourage my child to show me what he is interested in. I can learn a lot about him and what catches his eye, and what he is interested in by this. MOM OF BOY AGED 2 TO 4

> My son is turning into a thinking person and I enjoy letting him make decisions for himself and I also like giving him choices and having him choose. MOM OF BOY AGED 2 TO 4

> I like for them to feel like what is important to them and their wants are also important to me.
> MOM OF GIRL AGED 2 TO 4

> My daughter knows what she likes and therefore always voices her opinions and that's what we keep in the house.
> MOM OF GIRL AGED 2 TO 4

> I find my child's influence on purchases to be informative, opinionated, mature and thoughtful.
> MOM OF BOY AGED 5 TO 7

> I have two older sons and my 6-year-old knows their taste so he is very helpful when buying for them or his father.
> MOM OF BOY AGED 5 TO 7

> I don't want to waste money on stuff that my daughter does not like, so it is important what she thinks. Also, I like to buy stuff that makes her feel like she is important in making decisions too.
> MOM OF GIRL AGED 5 TO 7

Sometimes for a fragrance of a household cleaner, she would let me know if it has a very strong odor, and I won't buy it. She helps me with a lot of things I buy and she's only 7 years old and I think that's great!

MOM OF GIRL AGED 5 TO 7

He helps me stay current on all of the new products.

MOM OF BOY AGED 8 TO 11

I always want my son to feel he has a say in our household purchases.

MOM OF BOY AGED 8 TO 11

They are very specific about clothing, toiletries, etc. It is not worth the trouble to try and guess what is acceptable.

MOM OF GIRL AGED 8 TO 11

My children are very, very important in making decisions and give good insight into many purchases.

MOM OF GIRL AGED 8 TO 11

He gives me his opinion on what is good and what is not worth the money. He is very watchful of prices and lets me know when there is a good deal on something.

MOM OF BOY AGED 12 TO 14

His science fair experiment in fourth grade influenced which laundry detergent we now use.

MOM OF BOY AGED 12 TO 14

She's knowledgeable about trends from magazines. Her opinions are valuable; she knows the decision rests with us but her opinions are weighted fully.

MOM OF GIRL AGED 12 TO14

My daughter is very smart and I would always take her opinion into consideration. She enjoys doing the shopping with me.

MOM OF GIRL AGED 12 TO14

As you can see from the quotes above, it seems, that the 4i4l decision-making process goes from mom wanting to teach her child, to child becoming quite helpful to finally, child teaching or instructing mom.

Not All Moms Love the Help

To be fair, not all moms are delighted with marketer's efforts to "help" them to help their children. And, although the vast majority of quotes received during our study suggested a high degree of child influence, *not* all of them did.

Importantly, while moms many times look forward to engaging their children in the purchase decision, often they face a difficult task due to a failure on the part of marketers. As Dr. Daniel Cook, Ph.D., associate professor of advertising and communication at the University of Illinois-Urbana-Champaign found: On the one hand, they delight in giving their children the things they want and in allowing them to choose them; on the other, some mothers think of much of the kids' commercial marketplace as an undifferentiated, sometimes formidable obstacle which they have to overcome.

When it comes to food purchasing and licensed products, at times mothers expressed to Cook near hostility toward manufacturers as well as media companies. One 31-year-old mother lamented how early her children came to identify and prefer food products that had characters on the box:

> Or they'll have more options in mac 'n cheese. . . . Like, they'll have some of the characters but usually Schnucks [a local grocery chain] will have Crazy Noodles, SpongeBob, Scooby Doo. . . . Of course, the regular 33-cent-box of mac 'n cheese nobody wants . . . There's the character ones that have less pasta and then are more expensive. They tend to have more in the aisle with the little packages of things they have for kids.

This mother also reports having a difficult time with portion control of graham snacks because the children are so drawn to the characters that she cannot serve the snacks out of the box. The result is that "half the grahams are on the floor of the car and you vacuum out the back seat."

Kids Agree. They Have a Part in the Decision!

Kids basically agree with their moms regarding the degree of influence that they have. According to the most recent *Harris Interactive YouthPulse,* 84 percent of today's tweens say that they influence or decide on which groceries their families purchase. Almost one in four say they influence the vehicle purchased by the family. These numbers are all somewhat close to the figures reported by moms.

Kids aged 8 to 12 reporting influence	
Clothing/apparel	93%
Video/DVD	93
Video games	87
Groceries	84
Sports equipment	71
Vacation	62
Software	57
Vehicles	22
SOURCE: *Harris Interactive YouthPulse*	

And now, the last intangible of influence. How many moms bought themselves or their family *something* that resulted from seeing a TV ad that appeared in a program that she was watching because of, or with, her child? Think of all the adult or mom directed ads or sponsorships on PBS!

Not only are parents listening to their kids about what to buy, but also *where* to buy, especially when it comes to clothing and accessories, where more than 80 percent of parents agree that their child's preference is very or somewhat important in choosing which stores to shop in. Kids influence on their parents' online habits and purchases is also sizeable. More than half of today's parents said that their children influenced them to purchase a product from a website, and 42 percent have been influenced to click on an online ad, according to ClickZ Stats Demographics.

Through his research, Dr. Cook also found that, "When they can engage in cooperative, joint activities with their children, mothers tend to express their most positive feelings toward stores and consumer goods." For example, Cook found that planning for a birthday celebration was a particularly satisfying activity for mothers, in large part because it was undertaken in a spirit of mutuality. Mothers report actively engaging their children, sometimes as young as three but increasingly as they get older, in the planning of the event including the theme, the guests, the kinds of games played, party favors, and the kind of cake they will have.

One 32-year-old mother of two related how she engaged her 3-year-old in the preparations for her fourth birthday:

> I would say it was about the last six weeks or so before her birthday that we told her that her birthday was coming up and focused more. The birthday was at the very end of July. And so in June we sort of starting prepping her for her birthday, if you will, what did she want, what kind of cake did she want, what kinds of things did she want.
>
> She came with me to the bakery and the lady sat with her at the table and said, "What kind of cake do you want?" Of course, the chocolate. "What kind of filling do you want?" "Chocolate." She wanted to be very involved in the whole process. She filled the piñata, and picked out the candy she wanted . . .

There are also times in which mom will make a decision regarding her child because it makes *her* look good to her friends. Again, when it comes to birthday parties, Cook found that often birthday parties for pre-school and early elementary school children are as much about mothers' creativity and an orientation to other mothers, as they are about the child's desires. Some mothers gain quite a reputation in their social circles for putting on parties with innovative themes, party favors, and activities.

Birthday parties, along with Christmas and Halloween, enable mothers to co-create the context in which consumer goods, images, and icons are prominent. In this context, they are less threatening to the mother's role of gatekeeper to her child's world. They also help her demonstrate some of her skills and nurturing to her immediate peers.

This holds true for many categories. We've seen new moms buy the most expensive, status-oriented, baby carriages, clothing, and playthings, more as an expression to others than for any other reasons. After all, why buy a top-of-the-line baby carriage from Evenflo for $230, when you can buy a Bugaboo for $729!

And, let's not forget that "got to have" toy for her child, like Cabbage Patch, Super Soaker, or Tickle Me Elmo. When each of these became the "got to have" toy of the year, parents tried just about anything to acquire one. They would pre-buy one or call stores all over a city. Parents would offer bribes and wait in horrendously long lines, all in order to acquire something that was a symbol to others that they were being a good, attentive parent.

Children become an important influential part of the 4i4l consumer equation almost immediately. Studies have shown that pictures of children and babies evoke positive adult responses. When asked to choose between a picture of an adult and one depicting an infant, adults choose infants. As mentioned before, mom begins to make various changes in consumption for herself and her household as soon as she knows that she is pregnant. Alcoholic beverages go down; eggs, proteins, vitamins go up.

As newborns, children influence moms through their actions and reactions. One major stage occurs at 3 months of age. It is then when infants make concentrated eye contact and smile in response to a smile on an adult's face. When smiling occurs, a whole new emotional bond develops between infants and parents.

Moms have confirmed to Professor Cook that by two years of age, their children begin to recognize characters, even when some claim to have limited their children's media use.

Mom's Influence on Children

Obviously mom has a huge influence on her children. After all, she is the primary decision maker and can, if she so chooses, insist that her child do or not do something. She is the one with the money. She teaches her child much of what that child will understand about shopping for products and services. She is the provider, the choice-offerer, the asker. And, as discussed in Chapter 2, today's kids see their moms as valuable partners in life. She is the one a kid is most likely to go to for advice.

In our many years of researching moms and kids, here are the primary decision scenarios we have observed that are age related.

1. Mom introduces and influences trial, child influences repurchase.

When her child is an infant, it is mom that introduces her child to the world and its products and services. She is also the one who will decide just how much she will accept from the child in terms of an argument. Watch how a mom introduces her child to the wonderfully tasty world of baby food. It is mom that first introduces and therefore influences her child to try a spoonful of strained green beans. And then it's the child who, when he makes a face, spits it out and begins to act cranky, influences mom to not buy this product again!

Mom as influencer is an important way in which long-standing brands have a distinct advantage in remaining leaders in their category. Herein lies one of the secrets of the forever-popular Barbie Doll. Unlike just about any other toy, Barbie has found a way to stay new enough for retailers to remain committed to the line and aggressively merchandise it year after year, yet Barbie is familiar enough to moms so that they still identify with her.

The key here is "new enough." Retailers today demand newness in just about all items, and especially toys, if they are to remain committed to carrying the line. So, Barbie adds some new clothes, or some new activity, or some new friends and, as a result, she seems new and exciting to kids and retailers of today but is still the doll mom grew up with! And, as such, mom is more than a little biased about encouraging her daughters to buy into the Barbie world.

Today, we are seeing other toy retailers try to bring back many of mom's old favorites like Care Bears, My Little Pony, and Pound Puppies in order to enjoy a little mommy influence. However, they must learn from Barbie, and plan to keep the brand looking new and exciting in the coming years if they are to hope to maintain retailer commitment to the line over the long-term.

Consistent moms need to teach and nurture. It is mom who generally introduces safe, health-oriented, educational and other good-for-you products to her kids. As you can imagine, kid appeal here is virtually non-existent. However, if the child rejects, or if the mom even suspects that her child will reject, she may not buy!

Last, a particularly important part of mom influence is that although it may first occur during a child's younger years, this first influence can be a lasting one. Again, when thinking of Barbie, moms *of today* are influencing their daughters to try Barbie *as a result* of having been first influenced to try Barbie many years ago. This can be especially important for today's manufacturers because if a marketer successfully captures a new consumer as a child, then, once that child has grown to be an adult, she might help to introduce the next generation to its brand.

Studies have also confirmed that, in many cases, college-aged daughters' brand preferences are significantly influenced by the brand preferences of their moms. In 36 percent of families, mothers and daughters are found to buy the same brands, across all categories measured. This is more than twice the rate that would be explained by chance alone, according to an article in the *Journal of Marketing*.

So what does this mean? Naturally, there are times when marketers must have a primary target of mom, especially for products and services consumed primarily by infants and preschoolers. Communicating to mom in this case is essential. However, as a child ages it would be wrong to totally ignore the child.

For one thing, communicating to children through advertising and packaging will make it more likely that they will accept a product once moms introduce it. Moms have told us that they actually appreciate when marketers do this through products and communications targeted to their children because it makes it easier for them to convince their children to try (and like) various products. For example, according to the Yankelovich *Youth Monitor,* 75 percent of parents of 6-to-11-year-olds agreed that "Health and beauty aids made just for kids make it much easier to help my child develop good hygiene habits."

2. Child is the introducer *and* influencer

As children grow they become more influential in the entire decision-making process resulting in mom's role becoming more of an acceptor and rejecter. As kids become a little older, they naturally begin to exert their own influence whether by simply asking or telling, "I want that," pointing (usually to a recognizable character), grabbing, and so forth. As children grow to become tweens, their influence increases perhaps to the highest level among kids of all ages. It is at this age that kids more fully understand commercial messages and they are far more articulate in their desires. And, unlike kids that are even older, tweens lack the purchasing power to make significant purchases on their own causing them to rely more on their power to influence.

Marketers, whose products and services tend to enjoy this type of decision-making scenario, have an easy consumer target—the kid part of the 4i4l. All elements of the marketing mix, from the product, the price, the distribution and the communication must have the child in mind.

Again, rest assured that many moms actually appreciate it when manufacturers do their part to properly market to their children. In fact, the 2003 Yankelovich *Youth Monitor* reported that:

- 70 percent of all parents agreed with the statement: "It makes my shopping easier when my child knows what brand he or she likes."

- 50 percent of parents of 6-to-11-year-olds agreed, "Using foods created for kids make it easier to find things my child will eat."

As one of our moms put it:

I feel if they have a say when I buy something new, they are more eager to try it.

MOM OF GIRL AGED 8 TO 11

3. Child is introducer but mom is the influencer

Here lies the fate of products or services that cross the line in mom's perception of health, safety, or price. While none of these concerns matter to the child, mom is more likely to block this type of purchase even though the child wants this item. This type of situation can be uncovered in early concept testing, where we are likely to see a product receive an A among kids but an F among moms. This is a significant warning especially among Restrictive moms who will, many times, win the battle.

What do you do about this? Use research to better understand moms' concerns over the product and, if possible find a way in which to help them be more receptive to the basic idea. If it's a food, add some vitamins or other healthy ingredients; if it's a toy, add some safety features or developmental benefits, and most importantly, clearly call this out on your package. McDonald's recently embarked on a campaign to inform moms that they now use all white meat in their chicken nuggets. Think that was just to be polite? No. It was to try and assuage some of the negative influence mom might exert with their children who want Nuggets.

Moms can, of course, also be a positive influence on their children. When watching how a tween girl shops for clothing, we observed how mom will take her daughter to a certain retailer, either on her own or because the child has asked for a specific place. Then the girl will, on her own or with mom's help, choose various items. The final verdict however, almost always comes when the child tries on the clothes and *asks her mom what she thinks!*

4. Mom *or* child is the introducer or influencer

There are many times in which we find a product or service with benefits to *both* mom and the child. Both have reasons to introduce the product to the other, and likewise, either will accept.

One such product is Kid Cuisine, the leading frozen meal for kids aged 3 to 8. Moms love it for being a balanced meal (health) and a much-needed convenience that she knows her kids will like (simplicity and nurturing). Kids love it because it is fun for them to eat and it has their favorite foods. Kids also know this because it is advertised primarily to them.

These types of products give marketers alternatives. One can market primarily to the kids for efficiency (which we will explain in Chapter 10) or if budgets allow, marketing to both audiences.

Mom/Child Influence Differs by Product Category

Over the years, we have observed that in general, moms of children aged 12 and younger treat different product categories in one of four ways: Kid Pushed, Off the Leash, Mom Pushed, or Off the Radar.

- **Kid Pushed.** These are categories, which, due to heavy kid-targeted marketing and relevant appeal are those in which the child is the primary influencer and perhaps purchaser as well. Beverages, candies, toys, software, clothing can all be considered to be within this category.

- **Off the Leash.** This is where mom becomes the "Choice-Offerer" discussed in Chapter 3. For these categories mom might lead her child to a category, but lets the child make the final choice as to specific brand. This is a common occurrence in that it offers mom and her child a basic win-win scenario. Mom will take her child to the store's fruit snack section and then let her child decide on the ultimate item and brand. Mom will perhaps take her child to the frozen entrée section, maybe even the Kid Cuisine location within the frozen section, and then let her child decide on which specific meal to buy.

  I encourage him to choose the flavor or variety of item I was already planning to buy—fruit snack flavors, ice cream flavors, etc."
  MOM OF BOY AGED 2 TO 4

  I decide to buy yogurt for the kids; she might get to pick the brand and/or flavor.
  MOM OF GIRL AGED 8 TO 11

- **Mom Pushed.** These are the categories that mom really wants for her children, such as vegetables, fruits, perhaps hot cereals, healthy foods, educational software.

- **Off the Radar.** Here we have categories that neither mom nor child want. Probably like an accordion!

Naturally, determining where your particular brand category falls on this grid will help you to understand where the influence will come from, and that understanding should impact the type of marketing that needs to be done. Some quick examples:

4i4l Consumer Matrix

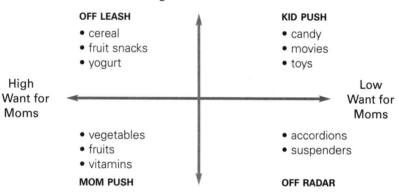

High Want for Kids

OFF LEASH
- cereal
- fruit snacks
- yogurt

KID PUSH
- candy
- movies
- toys

High Want for Moms ←————————————————→ Low Want for Moms

- vegetables
- fruits
- vitamins

- accordions
- suspenders

MOM PUSH   **OFF RADAR**

Low Want for Kids

- **Kid Push.** Manufacturers with items in this category need to be especially careful to market effectively directly to the child. Kids, here, are the introducer *and* the influencer. Mom is hands off and generally doesn't object to any kid moves here.

- **Off the Leash.** Here you should also market to the child at the very least through strongly appealing packaging. Knowing that kids generally look for products that they are familiar with or at least scream, "This one is for you!" the package should reflect kid-like graphics and if possible a familiar character or logo. If possible, you should advertise and promote to the child as well. Again, children are drawn to and want what is familiar to them, and advertising's main function to younger children is to enable them to recognize the product in the real world.

- **Mom Push.** Since mom is the primary force here, marketers must naturally appeal to moms first. However, in many cases this will be subject to kid influence in one way or another and since mom is already pre-disposed to categories in this quadrant, it would be especially helpful to moms if marketers would help her by doing whatever they can to make the specific item or brand appealing to kids. So, here too marketing to the child will help. Remember, moms are susceptible to their child's veto power. So the more you can do to limit this veto the better.

For example, during one particular situation we were looking at a new form of dental product designed for children. The concept was tested among both moms and children. Moms loved the item and stated positive purchase intent. Kids basically were OK with the item overall. As a result, the analysts proposed to this company that it market solely to moms since kids would not be motivated enough to positively influence moms. We believe that this could have been disastrous.

Upon further analysis, it was determined that the primary reason that moms liked the item was because of its proposed efficacy. The only doubts or dislikes that moms reported were that *they felt their children might not like it or use it!* What does this say? Mom was concerned about the probable kid veto! And, remember today's moms strive to simplify their lives so if they are concerned that their child will not use it, they will not buy!

The answer would be to let mom know that her child *will* use this new dental product. How? By packaging, naming, and advertising directly to their children in a way that a child might actually ask mom for it, or at the very least, endorse mom's decision to buy it.

As for the original dental hygiene concept scoring *just OK* to kids, well that tells you that you have to rethink how to present the concept to the child in a more favorable way. After all there are many different ways in which to motivate a child!

Fortunately, there are several examples of marketers helping moms with more push products. Most recently, we have seen new efforts to offer fresh fruit in more kid-friendly packages, or forms. Even McDonald's now has caramel dippers for apples! The cereal such as Tiger Power, by Kellogg's is another example of trying to make a healthier cereal more appealing to kids. And, Buddies by Johnson & Johnson is a fine example of making cleansing products more acceptable to toddlers and young children.

In summary, both the child and mom are important parts of the 4i4l decision-making process. Careful upfront research can help marketers better determine where the best chance of introduction might come from—the child or the mom, or both. Research will also help determine where potential red flags might hurt the influence. This in turn will prove important in helping today's marketers determine how to best approach the 4i4l. We will discuss some research options later in this book.

Implications

- Marketers should not ignore either the child or the mom in developing effective marketing strategies against the 4i4l.

- Marketers should think about the potential of kid influence and how to best harness it. Even when there is no point of difference you can make between your product and a competitor, you might be able to differentiate it to the child and therefore affect family preference.

- Because mom and child are literally joined at the hip, marketers must be wary of the kid veto halting mom from purchasing many items not only for the child, but also for the whole family. Marketers must also be wary of the potential influence children, and especially tweens and teens, have on purchases made for the whole family.

- There appears to be a segment of moms so sensitive to their children's input that their own purchases can be affected by their child. Imagine if a child thought a particular cleanser was better, or certain adult clothing was "cooler."

- Marketers have an opportunity to market directly to the child and thereby increase their influence behind their brand and capture share in those situations where a product or service or category is consumed by kids, even if kid influence is not particularly high.

- In those cases where the product or service is designed specifically for children you must market *to* the child first (and secondarily, if possible, to the mom).

- Tweens and teens are more responsive to the marketing of non-food items in particular (as opposed to younger children).

- Marketers should try to help moms that want to engage their children more by providing portion control, and clear product or branding differentiation on packaging.

- Since long established brand leaders have a distinct advantage as they enjoy stronger mom-biased influence, marketers of new brands would be well advised to promote to children in order to increase *their* influence or create a child veto. This is what the new Bratz dolls have successfully done recently against Barbie.

- It is important to properly research the potential decision making process of your particular product or service to best determine the optimum marketing mix.

- Careful research on new product concepts should be done to best determine if a potential kid veto or mom veto exists. If so, take corrective actions.

- One must determine where your product falls on the mom-child grid to best determine your ultimate target consumer.

6

The Mom & Kid 4i4L Consumer as a Market

How Many Products and Services Does the 4i4l Consumer Potentially Affect?

The primary reason that we are addressing this consumer is the vast number of products and total-dollar sales that are accounted for by the 4i4l. This could be sizeable considering that just about every product or service a mom and or child is involved with could be a 4i4l product.

As we saw in the last chapter, there are various foods, beverages, electronics and even household cleaners that now come to mind, but what about items like pharmaceuticals? Yes!

Imagine the mom of a sick child. The child is cranky, feverish, hurting. Mom is tired and stressed. And now, it's time for mom to administer just one, simple teaspoon of medicine to her poor suffering little girl. And guess what? It looks scary, and you can bet, smells and tastes awful. So what does the child do? Clamps her mouth shut, probably pushes the spoon away (no doubt spilling the medicine), pleading with mom not to make her take it. What happens? Mom either forgoes the medicine entirely or administers less than what is needed. At the very least, our pharmaceutical marketers have created a terrible consumer experience for both the mom part and the child part of our 4i4l consumer. Will the mom be open to an alternative medicine that might be better tasting and maybe packaged in a not-so-scary bottle next time? You bet!

What about services like eye-glass centers? Here too, imagine a mom that has to take her child to be fitted for eyeglasses. The child is probably a bit nervous—even reluctant. Mom is tired, stressed, and probably feeling at least somewhat guilty about this whole situation. Get the picture? The place is kind of sterile, maybe even a little scary for the child. Would mom be more open to a friendly, bright looking location that actually seems like fun for her child or that might even *reward* her child in some way for coming? Yup!

For eye-openers, at left is a list of many of the categories measured by Simmons, whose usage indexes high among households with kids. In every one of these, you can bet there is a heavy 4i4l consumer purchase dynamic present. If not, then a good marketing effort can certainly enhance it.

As we have said before, just because a certain category, or even brand, does not index highly to households with kids now doesn't mean it won't in the future. All it might take is for some product or brand to enter that category and begin to effectively market to kids. If kids find this new entry interesting, they could encourage purchase. For example, while frozen dinner entrée's indexes only average among households with kids, the brand Kid Cuisine indexes at 304! Probably at one time the yogurt category was a huge underperformer in households with kids, until brands like Trix, Danimals, and Go-GURT came along.

Categories skewing to households with kids aged 12 and younger	
Category	Index
Prepared lunch kits	206
Premoistened wipes	197
Toaster pastries	155
Camcorder/cameras	150
Frozen waffles	136
Frozen fried chicken	136
Sports drinks/quenchers	133
Pizza crusts (ready made)	133
Sloppy Joe preps	128
Meat snacks	128
Frozen hot snacks	126
Frozen breakfast entrées	125
Frostings	122
Pizza sauce	122
Packaged muffins	122
Snack cakes	122
Fruit juice	121
Dry soup mix	121
Frozen novelties	120
Breakfast pastries	119
Mexican food/ingredients	119
DVD players	118
Donuts	118
Nutritional snacks, granola	118
Frozen pizza	117
Brownie mix	117
Pancake mix	116
Canned pasta	116
Corn/tortilla chips	115
Instant cocoa	115

SOURCE: Simmons 2004

What Does this Market Look Like?

It's BIG! It is estimated that every three seconds a new birth occurs in the U.S., meaning that 11,000 new 4i4l consumers are born every day! And, of these births, 44 percent were to first-time moms. Also, more than one in three of these births are to single moms—twice the rate observed a decade ago.

In total there are 34 million moms with children under the age of 18 in their households—that is a number slightly *larger* than the entire population of Canada. And, even more impressive, there are 72 million children under the age of 18—and that is a number *20 percent larger* than the entire population of the U.K., France, or Italy! By the way, an easy way to remember about how many kids there are in certain age ranges is to figure about 4 million per year (the average U.S. annual birth rate, plus or minus a few). For example, when clients ask us the size of the kids market from ages 8 to 12, we can quickly estimate about 20 million, and we can divide it in half for coming up with just boys or girls.

Today's moms of kids under age 17 are predominantly white (63 percent), college educated (58 percent), and, although many would rather not, work full-time (50 percent).

While little seems to be different demographically among today's oldest and youngest GenX moms, there are at least two phenomena worth looking at. Specifically, younger moms tend to be more ethnically diverse and they are more likely to be stay-at-home moms. In looking at moms under age 35 (about half of all moms of children age 12 and under), we start to see a significant growth in the percentage of Hispanic 4i4l consumers. In fact Simmons data indicates that now more than one in five moms under the age of 30 are Hispanic.

Moms of children aged 17 and under	
White	63%
Black	16
Hispanic	15
Asian	5
Attended college	31
Graduated college	27
Employed full-time	50
Employed part time	18
SOURCE: Simmons Market Research	

Moms under age 35	
White	59%
Black	16
Hispanic	19
Asian	5
Employed full-time	43
Employed part-time	19
SOURCE: Simmons Market Research	

How Much Does the 4i4I Spend?

Children are expensive! Every time a mom gives birth to a new bouncing baby, she gives birth to a quarter million dollars of new debt! According to the *2004 USDA Expenditures on Children by Families*, it costs an average income family, $10,240 a year to raise a child. When factoring in future inflation, middle-income households can expect to spend an estimated $242,070 on a child *before* shipping him or her off to college. And if that's not expensive enough, remember that most moms have two or more children. (No wonder they are stressed!) For those who want to *save* money and decide to stop with just one child, there is a penalty anyway! The USDA finds that expenses per child in an only child family are 1.24 times that of families with multiple children.

Estimated Annual Expenditures* on Children Born in 2004

by income group, overall United States

| | | INCOME GROUP | | |
Year	Age	Lowest	Middle	Highest
2004	<1	$7,040	$9,840	$14,620
2005	1	7,250	10,140	15,070
2006	2	7,480	10,450	15,530
2007	3	7,890	11,070	16,370
2008	4	8,130	11,410	16,870
2009	5	8,380	11,760	17,380
2010	6	8,680	12,010	17,620
2011	7	8,950	12,380	18,150
2012	8	9,220	12,760	18,710
2013	9	9,460	12,990	18,960
2014	10	9,750	13,380	19,540
2015	11	10,050	13,790	20,140
2016	12	11,570	15,260	21,900
2017	13	11,930	15,720	22,570
2018	14	12,290	16,200	23,250
2019	15	12,550	17,110	24,810
2020	16	12,940	17,630	25,570
2021	17	13,330	18,170	26,350
Total		$176,890	$242,070	$353,410

*Estimates are for the younger child in husband-wife families with two children.

SOURCE: *USDA Expenditures on Children by Families, 2004*

If you think that $242,070 worth of costs per child is staggering enough, then you'll really be unsettled when you consider that this doesn't account for lost income that occurs when one parent decides to stop working for a while to raise the children, nor the additional $20,000–$160,000 costs of a four-year college education.

In an average family with about 2.1 kids, more than 40 percent of household spending is on kids' stuff. Actually, a Mom's Club survey found that 24 percent of moms estimate that they spend upwards of 70 percent or more of their total weekly spending on their children. About a third of total spending will go into housing; 15 to 20 percent will go for food; 14 percent transportation; 5 percent clothes; 7.5 percent healthcare; 11.5 percent school and 11 percent miscellaneous.

Estimated annual expenditures* on a child by husband-wife families

overall United States, 2004

Age of child	Total	Housing	Food	Transpor-tation	Clothing	Health-care	Childcare/ Education	Misc.
Before-tax income: Less than $41,700 (Average = $26,100)								
0-2	$7,040	$2,680	$980	$820	$350	$530	$1,020	$660
3-5	7,210	2,650	1,090	800	340	500	1,150	680
6-8	7,250	2,560	1,400	930	380	580	680	720
9-11	7,220	2,310	1,680	1,010	420	630	410	760
12-14	8,070	2,580	1,770	1,130	710	640	290	950
15-17	8,000	2,080	1,910	1,530	630	680	480	690
Total	$134,370	$44,580	$26,490	$18,660	$8,490	$10,680	12,090	$13,380
Before-tax income: $41,700 to $70,200 (Average = $55,500)								
0-2	$9,840	$3,630	$1,170	$1,230	$410	$690	$1,680	$1,030
3-5	10,120	3,600	1,350	1,200	400	660	1,860	1,050
6-8	10,030	3,510	1,720	1,330	440	750	1190	1,090
9-11	9,910	3,260	2,030	1,410	490	820	780	1,120
12-14	10,640	3,520	2,050	1,540	830	820	570	1,310
15-17	10,900	3,030	2,270	1,950	740	870	980	1,060
Total	$184,320	$61,650	$31,770	$25,980	$9,930	$13,830	$21,180	$19,980

continues . . .

Age of child	Total	Housing	Food	Transpor-tation	Clothing	Health-care	Childcare/Education	Misc.
Before-tax income: More than $70,200 (Average = $105,100)								
0-2	$14,620	$5,770	$1,550	$1,720	$540	$790	$2,530	$1,720
3-5	14,960	5,730	1,760	1,690	530	760	2,750	1,740
6-7	14,710	5,640	2,120	1,820	580	870	1,900	1,780
9-11	14,470	5,400	2,460	1,900	630	940	1,320	1,820
12-14	15,270	5,660	2,580	2,030	1,040	940	1,010	2,010
15-17	15,810	5,160	2,720	2,460	950	990	1,780	1,750
Total	$269,520	$100,080	$39,570	$34,860	$12,810	$15,870	$33,870	$32,460

Every year, considering that there are 72 million kids in our country, the 4i4l mom part of our consumer can be expected to spend about $737 billion on or because of her children. While we know that she will partner with her child for many of these purchases, at least one-third of this spending, the expenditures for food, clothing and miscellaneous will be highly influenced by the child part.

Annual spending on children for high kid-influenced items	
Food	$125 billion
Clothing	40 billion
Miscellaneous	80 billion

Now, how do we factor in the child influence we talked about in our previous chapter? Studies conducted several years ago by James McNeal, and others suggested conservatively that kids influence about 20 percent of all family purchases. Our new study suggests this estimate is too low; in fact, it seems to be the kid influence on products bought just *for adults*.

We can't help but believe that based on our recent study and all of the other research we have done on behalf of our clients, that kids influence at least 30 percent of all family expenditures remaining after expenditures made for taxes and for items purchased just for them. So, considering that there are 34 million households with children leaves us with an additional $379 billion.

And finally, there is the spending of the child itself. *Packaged Facts* reports annual tween (8-to-12-year-olds) spending to be $38 billion plus Harris Interactive reports of an an additional $94 billion.

What do they buy for themselves? Kids 12 and under tend to buy candy, games, food and clothing.

Interestingly, kid purchasing is now occurring online too! Parents of 70 percent of children aged 8 to 12 and 85 percent of teens say that their kids have participated in online purchases, according to EPM Communications.

Percent of 8-to-12-year-olds purchasing for themselves	
Candy	60%
Games/toys	57
Nail polish (girls)	41
Books	33
Soda/beverage	28
Snack	27
Clothing	25
Fast Food	14
SOURCE: WonderGroup and Kids Eyes, 2003	

Other Reasons that Kids Are a Major Part of Our Equation

They like to shop. One of the reasons today's 4i4l consumer has become so important is that kids often shop together with their moms. Seventy-nine percent of today's 6-to-11-year-olds shop at the grocery store at least some of the time; 36 percent report doing so most of the time. And, what is the favorite store for both boys and girls? Wal-Mart, of course, followed by Target.

Percent of girls aged 6 to 11 reporting as a favorite	
Wal-Mart	37%
Target	22
Old Navy	21
Limited Too	17
Payless Shoes	13
SOURCE: Kid Simmons, Fall 2004	

They have money. Not only do today's kids influence mom to make a lot of purchases whether for them or for others, but they also have a keen understanding of money and make quite a few purchases for themselves. The average weekly spend is $8.90 for kids aged 8 to 12 and a significant jump to $25.40 for 13-to-17-year-olds, according to Roper Reports. Kid Simmons says that 31 percent of kids aged 6 to 11 report getting weekly allowances and an additional 41 percent report getting money when they need it. In addition to allowances, kids get money from doing chores (52 percent), outside jobs (9 percent) and from parent and grandparent gifts.

Teens spending comes not only from what they earn but also from one of the most prevalent gifts they receive—gift cards. Ninety-one percent of boys and 95 percent of girls received at least one gift card during the past year and two-thirds have bought one as a gift for someone else, according to *PromoP:L*.

The resulting total?

The 4i4l consumer of today spends about $1.25 trillion a year!

$737 **billion** for children

$379 **billion** family purchases kid-influenced

$38 **billion** by tweens

+ $94 **billion** by teens

_____

$1.248 **trillion!**

Implications

- This is one *highly* important market to look at!

- The reality that almost half of a household's entire spending goes to kid-related costs confirms that a top factor in all of mom's spending and efforts must be the welfare of her children.

- Any marketer doing business in a category skewing to households with children has an opportunity to capture mom business by developing marketing efforts directly to children.

- You should carefully consider ethnic diversity, and especially Hispanic, when talking to today's moms.

- If you want to save money, do NOT have children! (Only kidding!)

- Bearing in mind that today's tweens and teens like to shop, retailers too must begin to aggressively address the kid part of our 4i4l.

7

How the 4i4l Thinks

BEFORE WE ENTER the second part of our book where we will discuss various techniques for marketing to the 4i4l, we believe it is important to address a topic of critical importance to the kid half of the consumer—how this half of our 4i4l consumer *thinks*.

We feel fairly confident that you, the reader, are an adult (despite what your spouse or friends may think of you). So, we think that you will have little trouble in being able to think like one and easily understand what a typical adult can and cannot comprehend.

But, since a significant portion of 4i4l marketing efforts may be targeted to the kid half of our consumer, you must fully understand just what this individual is truly capable of understanding. It is not very productive to spend a substantial amount of time and money mounting a significant advertising, promotion, packaging, or product development effort that totally misses the mark because the kid you were hoping to target says, "Huh?"

Before developing marketing strategies against your particular 4i4l you must first determine what age, or stage of mental development the kid part of your consumer resides in.

Essentially, the foundation for what a person can understand comes from two places: (1) the stage to which one's brain has developed and (2) the experiences that he or she has had. This is why it is so difficult for adult marketers to understand how to effectively market to children. The truth is: (1) the adult brain is just far more developed than the brain of a child and, (2) adults have experienced a whole lot more than kids have. As a result, because they are adults, marketers will often incorrectly assume that kids understand and relate to things,while in reality they cannot.

So, let's look at what kids can and cannot do or understand. Children's brains change dramatically in key areas up to and even past puberty. Until a recent 2000 study, scientists believed that brain development slowed after the first few years of life and the brain was basically organized by the time a child enters first grade. Now it is understood that changes still occur between ages 3 and 15.

One of the best ways in which to understand how the brain develops in children is to go back to the observations and teachings of developmental psychologist Jean Piaget (1896–1980). Piaget recognized four stages of cognitive development:

1. Sensory-Motor Intelligence (0–2 years old)

2. Pre-operational Thought (2–7 years old)

3. Concrete Operations (7–11 years old)

4. Formal Operations (11–15 years old)

While we have found that the age cut-offs are not as specific as Piaget first suggested, they do provide a good approximation of when cognitive abilities begin to change significantly. And, most importantly, the mind *must* pass through these stages linearly in its development. A child is not ever going to be capable of having the cognitive development of stage 4, without first possessing stages 1–3.

The Child Aged Birth to 2

This, the earliest stage of childhood, is a time in which there is a massive overproduction of synapses occurring in the brain and it is a period of high potential for learning. Kids become aware of the effect that their own actions have on the environment around them. By the time children are 9 months old, they can grasp items and put them in a grocery cart. By 12 months they can move their thumbs and fingers to grasp most objects. So, even for products used by these youngest of consumers, attractive packaging and colors become important.

From 12 to 18 months, children learn to experiment to see what the consequences will be. They can coordinate separate actions in order to achieve a goal. Moms see these actions and celebrate them, and encourage their children to learn more and more. It's a great time for marketers to be providing simple learning aids for mom to buy for her child. It's also a very important time to provide moms with assistance in child proofing their homes.

The Child Aged 3 to 6

Here is the child that gives marketers the hardest time. Because, here is the child that, when observed, *seems* to understand and appreciate far more than he actually does.

He talks! At this age, children's mental and social abilities are transformed by an explosive growth in their ability to comprehend and use language. By the time children reach about six years of age they have a vocabulary of between 8,000 and 14,000 words (although some parents might tell you that it is still limited to about three words, "I . . . WANT . . . THAT."

And because he talks, even at 3 years of age, he becomes capable of getting and holding an adult's attention in acceptable ways. Most importantly, he can begin to understand and communicate effectively, making him a far more proactive part of our 4i4l.

However, while he talks and may sound and look relatively intelligent, the fact is, he lacks the cognitive ability to think logically. He is bound by his immediate perception of what is real and he is extremely literal. Ads that show a certain beverage in orange but go on to say that it comes in many flavors, get credit from these kids only that it comes in orange, because *that's what they saw!* And woe to the marketer if those kids don't like orange. If a marketer fails to literally tell or show that their food product tastes great, kids of this age will not be willing to try it. Why? Because, kids *do not know* if it tastes good. Unless, of course, they have learned through previous experience with that product or another one that they see as the same.

As part of being bound by his immediate perception, our child of this age tends to be a victim of centration. **Centration** is a child's tendency to focus on one dimension or feature of an object to the exclusion of others.

The particular challenge here for marketers is to determine the *one* feature of your product on which you would like the child target to focus. For instance, we have seen many doll manufacturers who have offered dolls with many features such as eating and talking and wetting and crawling, only to see young girls focus on the fact that the doll's hair has a pretty bow in it. Years ago, we were fortunate to have the chance to market the Rosie Doll for a relatively small toy manufacturer. This doll did *one* thing. She sang ring around the Rosie when you touched her hands. Sure she was beautiful and her hair was combable and she came in several different hair colors, but the *one* feature we played up was that it sang ring around the Rosie. This doll became the Number One doll of the year against many multi-featured dolls manufactured by the major toy manufacturers.

Again, considering centration, you must be careful to craft very simple ads for this child, and make certain to minimize the chances that the child might focus on the *wrong* feature or element. One of our favorite learning experiences along this line came with a TV ad we did a long time ago for the Alvin and the Chipmunk's Deluxe Play House Set. The ad showed two girls carefully setting up the beautiful, well-detailed plastic home for Alvin and the Chipmunks and then carefully demonstrating (through their play), how they could have so much fun playing with their cute little Alvin and the Chipmunks figurines inside and out of it. Oh, yeah, to add a cute, soft element to the spot, we had a kitty interact with the girls. You guessed it, after showing kids the spot, all that they could talk about and truly remember was the cute little kitty!

As we will discuss in greater detail in Chapter 10, it is also because of centration that characters are so useful in advertising to kids this age—providing, however, that the character is clearly linked to your product. You know that kids will focus on the character, but since we want them to remember and understand that the character stands for your brand, it must be linked as literally as possible. A study by Macklin (1996) conducted among 3-to-5-year-olds confirmed that pairing visual cues with brands definitely helps younger children remember brand names. So, at least link your character visually showing the character interacting with your product. Better yet, name the character and the brand the same—Capt'n Crunch, Ronald McDonald, Kid Cuisine—hard to miss that connection!

Starting to better understand "centration?" Good! Now you'll understand why a child of this age will reach or ask for a package with a recognizable character on it. She wants "Angelica" from Rugrats! Never mind that Angelica is on a package of some food she will never eat. Or, she wants the "pink" package because she just loves the color pink.

Centration also plays a big part in how children of this age perceive brands. They don't! Studies have found that young children often discriminate between products on a simple heuristic of whether one particular quality (which may include a brand name, or a character) is present or not (Rust and Hyatt, 1991), or at best, typically one or two easily perceptible attributes (Bahn 1984, 1986; Diamond 1977; Shamir 1979). Other attributes or qualities of the product are of no concern to the child, as long as the primary "desired" characteristic is present. Think about this! Think of all those creative strategies that marketers and advertisers develop to make certain that the key message *and* all of the important reasons to believe or support points are communicated. Why bother? Kids only look for and understand the one simple heuristic they are looking for!

This can be a heartbreaker for many marketers. So many are "worried" that their "brand equity" will be diminished to their consumer younger than 7 if a licensed character appears too large on their package. What equity? Just recently, we were called by a business reporter asking us, isn't it important to get consumers when they are very young so that they remain loyal to your *brand*? HA!

Hey, children this age *are important*. They will certainly help mom decide what to buy. And they are certainly a nice-sized market themselves. **But they don't get brands nor are they loyal!** Children only gradually acquire the ability to distinguish between brands and between product and brand as they progress from kindergarten (5-to-6-year-olds) to third grade (8-to-9-year-olds) and then to sixth grade (11-to-12-year-olds). (Diamond, 1977) Also, when it comes to loyalty, young children frequently change preferences of favorite toys or foods and, if asked to name their favorite, may simply respond with the last toy they played with or food that they ate. (Capon and Kuhn, 1980) Adding further to this dilemma, studies by Rust and Hyatt (1991) found that stated child preferences are not even good indicators of future behavior.

Now, in truth, while children this age may not understand *branding* they certainly do recognize things like characters, colors, various names—and recognition and familiarity is very important to kids this age. According to James McNeal, author of *The Kids Market: Myths and Realities*, most children recognize the key attributes of a package, such as the logo, color, shape by the time they enter school. By the time that they are five years old, half of them are asking for specific brands by name.

Here also lies the secret power of licensing! Mickey Mouse can be anything, from a cereal, to a beverage, to a cup, to a bottle. The same holds true for a brand name among children this age. If a marketer wishes to determine how far he can stretch a brand name or what type of line extensions make sense, don't ask a young child! Because to a child there are *no* boundaries and there is *no* structure.

Another limitation of this aged child is that they are egocentric—they are incapable of understanding another's point of view. They could care less what others are doing or what products others have. It's only what *they* have or want that counts. "I am big." "I am six." "I am happy." "I want that." It is not until kids move to the next mental stage that this changes to "I'm bigger than most kids." "I'm happier than you."

For the most part, children this age are not able to mentally jump from one thing to the next. They basically see the world as one continuous story. Just ask a child around age 3 or 4 what they did for the day. She'll start out by telling you that she woke up, dressed, ate, and went to the zoo, saw this and that and yadayadayada. An older child will just tell you that she went to the zoo.

Commercials that use a lot of quick-cut action without a clear beginning and ending could go over the head of this aged child. Huston and Wright (1996) confirmed this after conducting several tests among young children and stated that unless subject matter is familiar, young kids have difficulty interpreting sequences of quick scene changes without transitions. Also, since they are incapable of mentally jumping back and fourth, if a commercial loses the attention of a young child, that child is lost for the rest of the commercial. It is not until children approach age 6 that their brains' frontal lobes have undergone some rapid growth, thereby enabling them to control their attention and actually plan new actions.

Tweens Aged 7 or 8 to 12

Welcome to the tween years. Tweens are too old to want to be considered "children," or especially a baby, but too young to do most anything else on their own. But, they can think more clearly, communicate more clearly and, as such, can better negotiate with their mom, making them a strong half to our mom side of the 4i4l consumer. Also, since at this age, parents can no longer expect "blind obedience" from their children, moms' socialization techniques become more indirect and increase their reliance on discussion and explanation, further binding the child even closer to the mom in the decision-making process.

This is the stage when a child can begin to apply logic to concrete problems. He no longer is bound solely by perception but can use thought as well to solve problems. He loses the egocentrism that bound him as a younger child and now, in fact, becomes extremely interested in being included with his peer group. In short, conforming to friends and not being excluded from groups becomes a major driver.

Importantly for marketers, this aged child acquires the ability to mentally order elements, so they can actually answer the various questions market researchers love to ask. They can group and classify, ascribing values to classes of people, events and objects and *this* could be the foundation of understanding brands and categories.

However, don't assume that the way in which a child categorizes or groups items in any way resembles the way that you would. For example, in one particular focus group session we asked kids aged 7 to 9 to sort a variety of pastries into groups or categories that made sense to them. One group sorted them according to what they felt were little-kids, big-kids, parents-type of pastries. Another sorted by chocolate vs. non-chocolate. Another sorted by what would be good to eat in the morning vs. the afternoon vs. the evening.

At approximately age 10, children begin to express simple preferences for branded products over non-branded. (McCormick 1988). Here, too, while this child seems to be pretty intelligent, marketers must be careful to understand their limitations. The primary limitation here is that these kids still have trouble dealing with abstraction. They still, for the most part, have to see something or hear something concrete for them to get it.

However, not only are their brains better developed here, but also their experiences are far richer than those of a preschooler. These kids are exposed to more schooling, bigger groups of school friends, and therefore more stimuli. For example, do you have to literally show or tell a child of this age that a certain fruit snack is delicious in your commercials or can you just have fun showing some strange new ways to depict the product? No and yes, because a child this age has probably already experienced fruit snacks and knows that they're very tasty and "classifies" all fruit snacks as tasty. But if the child has no prior experience then yes, we need to be far more literal.

Since experiences play an important part of how one processes information, it is not surprising that psychologists are beginning to ask whether the proliferation of media to which kids are now exposed, is affecting the way in which they can concentrate. The feeling is that as a result of all of the fast-paced media now available to kids, their developing brains may be becoming hard-wired to "multitask lite," as an article in *USA Today* named it, and they may be getting better able to cope with faster-paced, quick-cutting, multi-claim commercials.

The Teen Years

The teen years are a critical time to optimize the brain. It is the time in which sports, academics, or musical abilities will become hard-wired. Until recently, scientists believed that neural development in the brain was essentially organized well before the teen years. However, studies have now found peak growth rates in the middle and back of the brain associated with associative thinking and language occur up to age 15.

During the teen years there are immense changes that occur both physically and mentally but it is the advances in thinking and analyzing that are unparalleled by any other change that occurs to this segment. At this age, the kid part of our 4i4l can deal with possibilities, hypotheses, and abstractions. Unlike tweens, teens can deal with concepts that are not concrete or reality based.

To begin with the teen begins to develop reasoning skills. Reasoning skills can refer to thinking about and deciphering among multiple options and possibilities. It includes a more logical thought process and the ability to think about things hypothetically. Furthermore, the teen will begin to develop an abstract thought process about feelings such as trust, love, faith, intuition, and spirituality.

He or she also develops the ability to be introspective, or think in a process known as **meta-cognition.** Meta-cognition allows a person to recognize her own feelings and thoughts and then further interpret them.

Peers become more important to this age segment than to any other kid segment. High school students spend twice as much time with their peers as they do with their parents or other adults. And, just their luck, what differentiates the teen most from younger children is that because of their increased cognitive abilities, they now have the ability to imagine, and be concerned about, what others think about them. While a tween wants to be included and belong to a group, the teen is paranoid about being excluded, or ostracized by his or her group. The tween says, "I am right, but what do you think?" The teen says, "I know you think I'm wrong, so I probably am."

Because of this, self-esteem is a big part of their lives. Attractiveness heads the list, especially for girls, followed very closely by peer acceptance. Image is critical to them. A recent survey by BuzzBack Marketing Research finds that 95 percent of teens worry about their health and fewer than four in ten are happy with their current weight. What they do, say, wear, listen to, and watch all have perceived risks to these kids.

Teen activities are also dominated by puberty. While tweens are ruled by their need to fit in with their peer group, usually of the same sex, most teens are ruled by their need to attract and be accepted by the opposite sex. During this life stage, emotions and stress are heightened. Stratospheric highs, deep depressions, and the love of excitement are far more common. It's no wonder that the key target consumer for most theme parks today is the teen.

Implications

- Even in those instances where our 4i4l children are infants, marketers must do their best to understand how to please them.

- When advertising or marketing to the children's side of the 4i4l, it is advisable to either hire agencies and suppliers with kid experience or at the very least, immerse yourself in child psychology.

- Marketers can help teachers, educators, even clergy by providing them with methods in which to keep today's hyperactive, multitask-lite kids engaged.

8

Marketing to the 4i4l

NOW THAT WE KNOW more about the "who" our 4i4l is, what they do, what drives them, how they think, and how they go about making decisions, we can begin to look more closely at how to market to this super consumer.

While we are sure that many of our readers would hope for very specific plans and answers to the best way in which to market to the 4i4l, we unfortunately can only provide the options. The final plan and strategies must come from you, depending upon your particular product or service offering and, of course, your budget.

The purpose of our marketing efforts will be to activate our 4i4l consumer. We are not interested in entertaining it, teaching it, or just pleasing it. Rather, we want to motivate the 4i4l to do something concerning our product or service. We like to start with our activation model.

- Insight
- Intercept
- Engage
- Excite

Activation

In the next four chapters, we will discuss the key areas we believe you must consider in order to fully market to the 4i4l in a way that activates it.

Insight. To develop insight you need to do everything possible to get into the heads of our intended 4i4l. This is where our true opportunities lie. Before we construct our strategies we must know how super consumers think, what they may need or respond to, and how our kid half and mom half work together. This book will serve as an excellent start, but when it comes to your particular business challenge, we encourage you to do much more. **Chapter 9** will help you to do this.

Intercept. As we hope you can appreciate at this point in the book, our 4i4l consumer is quite busy and it is not easy for marketers to stop the 4i4l and capture its attention. This will be even tougher as your 4i4l consumer is actually beginning to *control* its media intake through Tivo, DVRs and the internet. **Chapter 10** will further show how the 4i4l consumer is barraged by all types of media so you will be armed with what you need to help you develop a strategy around cutting-edge media technology.

Engage. As we have learned by now, mom and kid have become extremely savvy when it comes to marketing. They have seen or heard it all and they have much more to do with their time than just stop and watch, listen, read, or click on your message, read your label, or spend any time at all actually thinking about what you are trying to tell them. When you are fortunate enough to have intercepted them through an effective media effort, you will get only seconds to engage them through your advertising and packaging. **Chapter 11** will help you to develop effective creative efforts that should engage the 4i4l.

Excite. Even once our *Insight* helps us to fully understand our target, and we have successfully *Intercepted* and *Engaged* our 4i4l, then we must continue to *Excite* our consumer. Today's 4i4l is surrounded by news, news, news. While the 4i4l will screen much of this out, this super consumer also expects and needs this excitement to stay interested in your brand. Whether it's promotions, new line extensions, or new messages, **Chapter 12** will take you there.

9

Developing Insights—Researching Your 4i4l

INSIGHTS ARE THE MOST valuable "currency" in marketing. It is from insights that you can create the best new products, the most relevant messages, the most effective media plans, and the best ways in which to keep your brand interesting to today's demanding 4i4l consumer.

Insights can come from anywhere. You can acquire insights by simply keeping up with the findings and news that others are reporting about today's moms and kids. Much of the kid media and major mom publications regularly conduct their own research and will usually share their findings with prospective clients. Insights can also come to you by keeping abreast of marketing and media news. Some excellent reports and newsletters include:

- **AOL.** AOL is an online service provider and is by far the most successful proprietary online service with more than 32 million subscribers at one point.

- **Cynopsis.** This is a free daily e-mail presenting the latest news pertaining to kids and kids entertainment programmers. Kids entertainment trends are especially highlighted here.

- *Parents* **Magazine Research.** As a new parent, you want the best advice possible. For over 75 years *Parents* magazine has been the source so many parents and parents-to-be to rely on.

- **Roper** *Youth Reports.* Roper *Reports* deliver the most up-to-the-minute view of the consumer marketplace. Its nationally representative database is comprised of tens of thousands of annual consumer interviews and is balanced to the most current U.S. Census report.

- **Simmons.** Both Simmons Adult and Kid Simmons are updated quarterly and available by subscription. They report attitudes, activities, and product/brand and media usage.

- **Yankelovich** *Youth Monitor.* Yankelovich delivers measurable breakthroughs in marketing productivity for its clients. It has a unique database and segmentation solutions, plus unparalleled information-based insights into consumer motivations and lifestyles. It also identifies specific, tangible opportunities for competitive advantage by moving clients from simplistic targeting to advanced productivity solutions.

- *Youth Markets Alert* published by EPM Communications. This twice-monthly newsletter presents summaries of research findings, newsworthy activities, and other relevant facts pertaining to today's youth and youth marketers.

- *Youth University.* Youth University (YU) is a bi-monthly e-zine published by WonderGroup. This e-zine summarizes and adds perspective to some of the bigger stories concerning kids, tweens, and teens that have occurred during the prior weeks, including some of the research findings conducted by the agency itself.

Andy Scheurer, Vice-President, and General Manager of Launch-Force, a leading new product development agency, says, "to find insights you must look and listen all the time, not just in a focus group of consumers. Discovery of insights requires viewing from multiple perspectives. They seldom present themselves head-on." Consumers rarely articulate an insight directly, completely, or succinctly.

That is not to say that there is no room for traditional qualitative research like focus groups; it's just that we caution that these must be handled carefully. Why the caution?

- Rarely will a mom or a child know why they actually do something, let alone what they are actually doing, and as far as accurately remembering things like "when" or "how many times," be very careful. We can't tell you how many times we *ask* a mom what she has bought or used for herself or for her kids, only to later do a pantry check and find totally different products than what she *remembered* using.

- When looking for unfilled needs, don't bet on a mom or child telling you this. Rarely if ever have we heard this expressed as an answer to a simple question. But, *present* a mom or a child with a new concept that comes from an insight you've generated elsewhere (like by some intuitive feeling you've developed from observing the marketplace) and, surprise, they might tell you they *need* this. Hey, this wasn't an unmet need before!

- Kids need to feel like they belong and they don't like to be "wrong." So expect a lot of bias in a group. Watch carefully and you'll see kids change their vote or opinions to match that of another child.

- Also, because kids are insecure and don't like being wrong, they are particularly reluctant to offer a true prediction of the consequences of something new. Try to gain insights from tween girls as to what next year's back-to-school fashion might look like and you'll get nowhere. We tried this, and we got nowhere. Instead, watch *how* they pick up on fashion and how they talk about it, and *then* you'll get some interesting insights!

- Last, try as they might, moms or kids just aren't brand managers. Asking them to design, create, or predict is very tough for them. Otherwise they would have your job! Here, too, it is often better to have them react to something you have in mind.

Tips for Focus Groups

So how do you deal with these cautions? Melissa Morrison, director of consumer insights for LaunchForce gives us some handy tips:

- Get respondents to think about and concentrate on the topic *before* coming to research by giving them homework. Kids, especially, take homework very seriously and generally do a great job preparing their homework prior to your research group. Homework could be anything from taking pictures, making drawings, collages, or answering simple questions relative to the topic that will be discussed in the group. Not only does this help the participants remember more clearly, but also the homework often presents new insights.

- When asking moms about products for their children, you must usually take the step of reminding moms to "put their mom's hat on." Moms today are so in sync with their kids' wants and habits that you must be sure that you know whether mom is expressing her own opinions or those of her child.

- Consider having respondents keep a diary prior to the groups. This is especially useful in helping them remember what they actually did pertaining to your product and when they did it.

- When asking simple yes/no, like/dislike questions especially to kids, have them "cover their eyes" and raise their hands. At times, we'll give them a red, yellow, green card to "secretly choose" and then hold up for their answers. This helps prevent bias and gives kids permission to disagree with each other in a fun, non-threatening way. Then let the discussions begin!

- In questioning children under age 8 it is better to have them react to specific, concrete questions rather than have them imagine or create answers and situations. Remember what we saw earlier. Young kids' thinking abilities center around things that are "concrete" not "abstract."

- When dealing with kids, it is best to get them to contribute as quickly as possible and involve them in becoming active participants. If, at the start of a group, you spend too much time talking to them, kids might become passive.

- Keep boys and girls in separate groups. Girls will try to play to boys and try not to look wrong, especially in the eyes of boys. Boys try to act too macho or disinterested to play up to the girls.

- For kids, keep ages or grades within two years. Again remember kids do not like to be wrong, and they will generally defer to older kids. Also, remember that older kids (tweens) do not want to be considered babies, so do not put them in the same group with younger children. Plus, a three-year age span is a huge range in the world of kid development and experiences.

- Be mindful of what kids can and can't do by age. Don't expect younger children to be conceptual. Provide stimuli to help kids understand concepts until at least 12 years of age. Don't ask them to "rank" at a young age. "Yes" or "no" is hard enough.

- If appropriate, include product sort exercises in mom or kid groups when trying to determine how the 4i4l approaches various categories. For example, for candy, we saw kids sort by: "for kids" vs. "not for kids." Others sorted by "chocolate" vs. "fruity." Moms sorted by "healthier" vs. "not healthier." Once they have helped you understand the criteria by which they approach the category, you can then see how they rate each brand accordingly and look for opportunities and insights.

- Having kids draw pictures or collages pertaining to an experience, or a brand will tell you more than what you could learn by simply asking questions. In general, kids love to draw and perform arts and crafts. In one case, we asked 8-to-12-year-olds to give us a drawing or collage representing eating dinner with one of their favorite brands. What we, along with our client, saw surprised us. Almost every picture clearly had the brand's character prominently displayed. What was truly surprising was that this character hasn't been used in advertising for years and currently plays only a very small role on the package. The insight: Kids really identify positively with this brand's character. The recommendation: Bring him back in advertising and more prominently on the package.

- If probing kids to find their feelings or opinions about a subject like a specific character or brand, it is often helpful to have them express their feelings in a drawing or collage so you understand what *they mean* by certain words.

It MAKES ME FEEL Happy. YELLOW. It is good to be happy because it's better for people to be arround me when I'm happy

For example boys and girls aged 8 to 12 from around the country were asked to tell us what a specific word means to them. We asked them to write and/or draw how it makes you feel, what you're doing when you feel like that, what color it might be.

In this situation we learned that "Happy" is what you would expect, but there is an interesting twist on the interpretation—"*It is better to be happy because it's better for people to be around me when I'm happy.*" Some unexpected meanings we heard:

- "Lazy" is a sad thing to be.
- "Popular" is a mixed bag—two sides to this coin!

Here is one more important caution about qualitative research involving kids. The good news is that kids generally love participating in research. They are truly excited to have their opinions heard and can't believe that they are actually being listened to and even paid.

The bad news is that kids can be bitterly disappointed if, after being recruited, they do not get the chance to participate in the research. Researchers generally over-recruit children in order to help ensure that an adequate number of respondents show up for the groups. Once the researchers have filled their quota they might simply just send the rest home. We have found that, even when paid, this is very disappointing to those who are not taken. It not only alienates the child, but the mom too! Therefore, we recommend that you have another set of simple questions that these children can fill out.

Even if it takes just a few minutes of their time, it will make them feel important and let them and their moms leave feeling very satisfied. Plus, if your questions are good, you will get some additional valuable information!

Other Techniques for Mining Insights

When mining for insights there are other qualitative techniques that might prove even more beneficial. Specifically, rather than typical focus groups, consider:

Friendship pairs. Friends will remind each other what they do and will also encourage more truthful answers since the child knows that her friend is there to confirm or deny what is being said.

Sibling pairs. Siblings keep each other remarkably honest plus they have such a strong rapport and comfort level with one another that they easily ignore the biasing factor of a moderator. Separately, these pairs are especially helpful in trying to generate insights about younger children. We have found that the *best* interpreter for what young children are trying to communicate is an older sibling.

Mom/kid pairs. This is especially valuable for getting insights into how mom and child go about making decisions or carry out a task regarding your category. For example, if you are interested in how a 4i4l is going to decide on shopping for back-to-school clothing, you might just explain to a mom and child, "OK we are going to go shopping for clothing. Now just act out how you might decide where to go or what to get." Then simply stand back and watch what happens. You will see for yourself the dynamics of who is doing what.

Also, if merely asking direct questions, you will notice a new degree of honesty. Watch the reaction of each to the answers the other gives. In one particular situation we had asked a mom and her child what they thought of the hotel they had stayed in at a particular resort. The mom said: "Sure, we loved the hotel we stayed in." Her child immediately gave her a questionable look whereby the fun began and the *real* answer came forward.

Remember that insights come from observing not just listening, so at the conclusion and debrief of any qualitative research make sure that you have asked yourself and everyone else observing the research not just what they heard, but what did they *see* and *feel* when watching the research.

Observation

A great way to come up with insights is through simple observation. Keep your eyes and ears open, know where to look and listen, *and* have a consumer and purpose in mind. Here are some suggestions:

Mall Tours & Insight Walks

Visit a mall with no consumer or purpose in mind and all you'll see is a lot of stores and people. In one case, we were visiting mall stores with our minds focused on the tween part of our 4i4l for the purpose of developing new beverages. One particular store we visited was Bath & Body Works, a favorite location for tween and teen girls. Looking over the names of all of the lotions and soaps, their colors, and the girls' reactions gave us our insight for an entirely new flavor and color beverage in an entirely new container.

Again, with your mind focused on your target consumer or other marketing purpose, go on a walk, but make that walk in a place where you will see and observe lots of moms, or kids, or moms and kids. Visit Chicago and see American Girl, Nike, Crate and Barrel, the Pier. Walk with a purpose in mind and look at how people are reacting to one another. Observe the colors, packages, flavors, smells, and actions and look for insights.

Blog Buzz

One of the best things about the internet is that it allows people from all over the world to communicate with one another. An even better thing for marketers and researchers is that it allows *them* to observe what all of those people communicating on the internet are saying! Whatever your task at hand, search for some blogs that might be relevant and begin to monitor them. See what others are talking about regarding your category, brand, or challenge or simply what they are talking about regarding their lives. Again, you *will* develop insights.

In Home

Observing kids and moms in their homes can also be a wonderful source of relevant insights. And here is a big hint. You don't even have to be there to do it. We're not talking about hidden cameras or sneaking around in the bushes either. One particular insight that we picked up years ago is that kids and moms are more than willing to try to help marketers and, at least they try to be honest in what they do.

Considering this, we have been very successful in giving moms and kids video cameras to use and record what they are doing when they are engaged in an activity in which we are interested. In one particular case we wanted to know what goes on when mom decides what to serve her kids for dinner. The videos candidly showed arguments and even questionable hygiene habits more honestly than if we were actually present. What they also gave us was an insight into how some moms would literally present a choice of meal solutions to their kids and ask them to make the choice. It was not unheard of to have one child in the family choose one thing, another child choose something entirely different, and mom just complied. The result? We developed an insightful ad campaign for one of our clients.

Create Environments

Another way in which you can develop insights is to create environments in which to observe kids or moms doing things relevant to your particular project. For example, when working on a specific assignment involving the development of a new condiment, we set up several "stations" whereby kids were given various creative assignments. In one particular station we provided kids with lots of food stimuli like sprinkles, candies, glitter, pop rocks, and endless other objects. The insight, when thinking of condiments was that kids really love to decorate their foods with certain things. The result? We helped developed Heinz EZ Squirt Green Ketchup.

We did the same exercise to gain insights into how kids would work with a particular line of colored glue by Elmer's Glue. Kids found the color interesting but once used to glue together two things, the color made no difference. We could have asked kids all types of questions, but in watching them work with this and other artistic media we found *the* insight. Specifically, kids are fascinated with 3-D, multi-dimensional art. Unlike other media, glue comes out raised from the page and it dries that way too—giving it a 3-D look. We also found the mom insight that "glue" is for pasting *not* for coloring. The result? Re-naming, re-packaging, and re-positioning Elmer's Colored Glue to Elmer's 3-D paint pens. This move resulted in a more than tripling of the business and proved to be a foundation of an entire line of products for Elmer's.

Hire a Pro

While this might sound like a self-serving pitch for companies like ours, there is significant value in taking advantage of the versatility and experience that the right outside help can bring.

It brings versatility. Marketing pros that have had the opportunity to work in more than one category will readily tell how their experience in my category helped them be smarter in the next one. Way back in our consumer package goods marketing days, I moved from being a marketing director for a confectionery company to a marketing executive for a household cleaning products company. As a result, I was one of the first household cleaning products marketers to ever offer retail promotions, something previously unheard of in that category. They were highly effective and unique to *that* category but, in truth, they had long existed in the confectionery market. Also, did you ever hear about the many consumer package goods marketers that moved into business-to-business marketing? Many became super stars merely by doing in b-to-b what they had been doing for years in consumer package goods categories.

It brings a wealth of experience. The advantage of hiring a professional marketing agency experienced in looking for consumer insights is just that. You're getting a huge jump-start on experience! A company like this already comes to the table loaded with insights that they have seen from all of the other work that they have done. Insights that might have been developed for toys can also prove to be helpful in foods. Cereal insights can help in pharmaceuticals; health and beauty insights can help in beverages, and so on. As an example, in reviewing a new product concept for a pharmaceutical company, we were able to use an insight acquired from working with another category to quickly determine that the pharmaceutical concept could be modified in order to make it significantly stronger.

Said another way, looking for insights by yourself, or within the box of just the experience that you or your company possesses, can be truly limiting. Bringing in some pros with various experiences will help your company gain some true "out of the box" insights.

10

How to Intercept Your Consumer— the 4i4l and Its Media

WITH RARE EXCEPTIONS, most marketers will not be able to afford the few expensive media alternatives that reach both mom and kid simultaneously. Prime-time TV programming or other mass-media vehicles are just too costly for most of today's advertisers. In Fall 2005, one 30-second ad on *American Idol* cost more than $500,000. So, how do we best intercept our 4i4l consumer considering that, in most cases, the mom part and the kid part have very different media habits?

To learn how to best intercept our 4i4l, we first have to understand the media habits of both the kid and the mom.

Today's Kids and Media

As we mentioned earlier, the media environment of the kid side has changed considerably—even over the past five years. The most recent Kaiser Family Foundation Study on media in the lives of 8-to-18-year-olds states:

> Five years ago, our examination of young people's media environments led us to characterize children's households as 'media rich.' The findings from 2004 point to a need for an even stronger term, that is "media saturated."

There is now an immersion of America's very youngest children, actually almost from birth, in the world of electronic and interactive media. Prices of computers have dropped substantially, high-speed internet connections have become prevalent, affordable digital recorders have been introduced, DVD players, digital music downloading, music file sharing have all become commonplace. Now even powerfully attractive internet programming, blogging and podcasting have materialized. All of these developments have reshaped, *and will continue to reshape,* the media behavior of today's youth.

Today's children tend to grow up in houses containing 3 TVs, 3 CD/tape players, 3 radios, 3 VCR or DVD players, 2 video game consoles and a computer with at least a 30-percent chance of its having high-speed internet access.

In just the past five years, among 8-to-18-year-olds, computers in the home have increased by 13 percentage points to 86 percent. Also, over these same five years, internet connections have grown by a phenomenal 30 percentage points to 74 percent, according to the Kaiser Family Foundation study.

Not only has the media environment changed within the homes of today's kids but kids' *personal* ownership of media devices has increased in virtually all areas, so much so that the majority of today's kids now have personal media both in their bedrooms and in portable forms. As of 2004, personal ownership of media was reported as follows:

Personal Media Ownership: Total Sample and by Age

Percentage of children whose bedrooms contain

MEDIUM	8-to-18-year-olds 2004	8-to-18-year-olds 1999	8-to-10-year-olds	11-to-14-year-olds	15-to-18-year-olds
TV	68%	65%	69%	68%	68%
VCR/DVD	54	36	47	56	56
DVR	10	—	8	13	9
Radio	84	86	74	85	91
CDs/tapes	86	88	75	89	92
Video game	49	45	52	52	41
Computer	31	21	23	31	37
Cable/satellite TV	37	29	32	38	40
Premium channel	20	15	16	21	20
Internet	20	10	10	21	27
IMing program	18	—	9	17	27
Telephone	40	—	31	39	50

Percentage of children with their own

MEDIUM	8-to-18-year-olds 2004	1999	8-to-10-year-olds	11-to-14-year-olds	15-to-18-year-olds
Cell phone	39%	—	21%	36%	56%
Portable CD/tape player	61	—	35	65	77
MP3 player	18	—	12	20	20
Laptop	12	—	13	11	15
Handheld videogame	55	—	66	60	41
PDA	11	—	9	14	8
Handheld internet device	13	—	7	15	17

SOURCE: "Generation M: Media in the Lives of 8–18 Year-olds," (#7251), The Henry J. Kaiser Family Foundation, March 2005.

Furthermore, while the youth of today have access to more media, parental supervision does not appear to have kept pace. Parental rules about the amount of time or type of content is enforced in less than 15 percent of homes among 7th to 12th grade students.

When looking at the types of media kids are actually using, the first thing that jumps out is that TV is still king and, in fact, there has been very little shift in youth usage of this medium over the past five years. As shown, 8-to-14-year-olds spend more than three hours a day in front of a TV.

Videos and DVDs have now become a staple of kids' lives, even down to the very youngest. Not surprisingly, according to the Kaiser Family Foundation, Fall 2003 *Electronic Media in the Lives of Infants, Toddlers and Pre-schoolers* report, in a typical day, almost half of all children aged 0 to 6 watch a video or DVD and on average, this age group spends almost as much time (38 minutes) viewing this medium as older kids.

Media Consumption

SCREEN	8-to-10-year-olds	11-to-14-year-olds	15-to-18-year-olds
TV	3:17	3:16	2:36
Videos/DVDs	:53	:46	:44
Movies	:31	:23	:21

SOURCE: "Generation M: Media in the Lives of 8–18 Year-olds," (#7251), The Henry J. Kaiser Family Foundation, March 2005.

PRINT	8-to-10- year-olds	11-to-14- year-olds	15-to-18- year-olds
Books	:27	:21	:24
Magazines	:12	:15	:13
Newspapers	:04	:05	:07
AUDIO			
Radio	:29	:57	1:15
CDs/tapes	:30	:45	1:09
COMPUTER			
Games	:20	:17	:19
Websites	:08	:13	:19
Chat rooms	:03	:04	:03
E-mail	:02	:05	:06
IMing	:03	:18	:27
Graphics	:02	:04	:05
Total computer	:37	1:02	1:22

SOURCE: "Generation M: Media in the Lives of 8–18 Year-olds," (#7251), The Henry J. Kaiser Family Foundation, March 2005

Audio, including radio, has long been a staple of American youth. It is a well-established fact that kids especially define themselves by the music they listen to. Many kids will even tell you that they decide pretty quickly if a commercial is truly relevant to them based on the music within the spot. Disney Records Vice President of Marketing, Damon Whiteside, states "Eight years ago, we considered kids' music to be anything that would appeal to ages 0 to 12. Today, it's much more segmented—roughly 0 to 2, 2 to 6, and 6 to 12." Audio becomes even more important to teens, and TV viewing drops versus the younger kids, possibly due to teens' greater mobility. Teens, aged 15 to 18 spend almost 2.5 hours a day with radio, CDs and tapes— almost as much time as they do with TV.

The challenge with audio as an intercept vehicle, however, has long centered on the fact that it is, in many cases, background in nature, or that kids will change stations immediately once commercials are on. The challenge is even greater now that kids prefer recorded music.

However, now a new audio challenge *and opportunity* is beginning to surface—Podcasting. A **Podcast** is an audio recording posted online and is like a radio show. It's free and you can listen to it whenever you would like. The challenge for marketers is the clutter. Because anyone can make a Podcast, there are thousands of them with no limit in sight. In July 2005, iTunes began offering users the ability to more easily find, subscribe to, and download them.

While podcasting adds even more to the nightmare of media fragmentation, it also provides an opportunity for marketers to do their own podcast, promote it, and offer it to consumers. In a sense, marketers can now do (and of course sponsor) their own shows, just like the old soap operas!

The media use that has changed most for kids over the past few years is, of course, their computer activity. Not only are there now more homes with computers but also there are more relevant, interesting computer activities to capture kids' attention—more online content, better websites, chat rooms, and so forth. The internet has emerged as the new playground for children. Now accommodating every leisure activity possible including music downloading, radio, online shopping, and the infamous AIM, it seems almost unnecessary to have to leave your computer, no matter what kind of entertainment you want.

Shown at left are the top ten internet sites most visited by 2-to-18-year-olds in mid-2005, according to the Center for Media Research.

Looking at some of these sites provides us with indications of marketing opportunities. For example, at least two sites, *Originalicons* and *Iconator* involve downloading or uploading fun icons. An icon is a visual image that kids can use on their instant messages or e-mail as a form of self-expression. Kids love icons so here is just one opportunity: Marketers can create icons of their brands, characters, logos or any

Top ten internet sites visited by 2-to-18-year olds		
Site	Unique Audience Composition	Unique Audience (000s)
Originalicons.com	80.0%	354
Iconator	79.7	577
Zenhex.com	77.8	629
Crush007.com	75.1	377
Myscene.com	73.8	902
PLyrics.com	73.6	435
eCRUSH	73.0	416
QuickKwiz	72.7	621
Buddyprofile.com	72.3	910
Picgames.com	72.0	333

Percentages are rounded.

Source: "Peer Pleasure: Teens Connect," Center for Media Research, 2005 symbol that rewards the kids with something really fun or cool *and* also reminds them of the brand.

Two sites involve finding "secret" crushes for tweens and teens and include fun, sort of innocent dating and matchmaking tips, chats, and so forth. Are there marketing opportunities around this that might involve advertising or promotion themes? Certainly!

Perhaps the most profound newest offering on the internet is the very recent emergence of the Webisode where kids can go online and view an animated, or even highly produced, live-action episode of a show available only on a specific, marketer-sponsored site. Here, truly is the soap opera of the new Millennial! For those of us old enough to remember back to the early days of electronic media, Procter and Gamble created and produced its own shows in order to have a vehicle for its advertising (hence the soap opera).

About five or six years ago Tiger Electronics, a very forward thinking toy company, saw the opportunity to create its own "comic-strip"—like web-based episodes—well before any other marketer conceived of this idea. Like most toy companies, Tiger realized that if it could provide a storyline for the company's new line of action figures (much like kids knew the story behind GI Joe, Star Wars, and so forth) kids would want to buy them. In what seemed to be a brilliant move, rather than having to pay millions of dollars creating and placing shows which told the story of these toys on TV, it instead created simple animated shows and placed them on the web. Great move. Wrong timing! Their idea was, in fact, brilliant. It was just way too soon. Not enough kids were online!

But now, kids *are* online and now animation techniques are extremely inexpensive. You can bet we are going to see a lot of company-sponsored webisodes in the near future.

MyScene

A very interesting site already providing company-sponsored content is MyScene. This is a Mattel site that centers on its My Scene doll line. Here girls can see merchandise, play games, and most importantly, become totally involved with the product and brand by view-

ing new animated stories concerning the characters. Take note of the "Check out the official movie site!" which allows the user to view the webisodes.

This site is particularly good at creating an immersive environment. Take note of the "my Shows" button which allows the user to view a series of webisodes featuring the characters in the site which are the same characters available as dolls.

Another example of using immersive story telling as a way to accomplish branding and marketing online is Target's new initiative. TV ads ask teens to watch episodes on oddsagainst7even.com.

Top online activities

Kids 5–9

Playing games

Schoolwork

E-mail

Kids 7–12

Play games

Listen to music

Watch videos, movies cartoons

Get information on celebrities

Get information on movies & TV

AIM

Teens 13–19

Download music

Online shopping

Watch music videos

Listen to internet radio

AIM

Get information on celebrities

What is particularly important to marketers is that not only does the internet provide a source of amusement to today's youth, but it has also morphed into a new form of communication. It has become a key way in which kids can connect with their peers and with a *brand*. Statistics show that 93 percent of kids aged 13 to 17 are IM users, and 10 percent of tweens have their own personal websites. Kids of virtually every age e-mail or IM and actively use the internet for acquiring information.

As a result, never before has kid word of mouth become such a huge force. Marketers are now trying to tap into this with the use of buzz-marketing efforts, trying to seed positive word of mouth and motivate kids to spread it throughout the internet.

Further, once kids become teens, online shopping begins to become more commonplace. So it is not surprising that online apparel retailers are targeting teens in a big way. Over 70 percent of teen internet users reported to have visited at least one retail category site in January 2005. Specialty apparel retailers targeting teens are among the retail sites with the highest composition of 13-to-17-year-old users. Many of these sites use tactics such as promotional enticements to persuade teens to make the brand part of their everyday lives.

Top retail properties by composition of visitors aged 13 to 17, January 2005

Total U.S. home, work, and university internet users, in thousands

	Unique Visitors Age 13–17	Composition UV Age 13–17	Composition Index
Total internet population, age 13-17	14,243	8.8%	100
Retail category visitors, age 13-17	10,137	7.7	88
Hollister.com	192	29.6	338
Hottopic.com	235	26.9	307
Babyphat.com	114	24.7	281
Alloy.com	585	22.4	255
Pacsun.com	149	21.9	250
Ae.com	313	17.5	199
Abercrombieandfitch.com	205	17.1	194
Cduniverse.com	128	14.7	168
Musiciansfriend.com	198	14.5	165
Foot Locker sites	313	13.8	157
Ebgames.com	150	13.6	155
Nflshop.com	114	13.0	148
Bartleby.com	153	12.4	141
Shoes.com	114	11.8	135
Roxio, Inc.	315	11.5	131

SOURCE: comSource Media Metrix, January 2005

Total computer activity among kids has more than doubled since 1999 and most of this increased activity has centered on more game playing, website visitation, and Instant Messaging. Interestingly, Instant Messaging was not even available five years ago, and now it accounts for an average of 38 minutes a day with about a quarter of today's young people using it daily.

Internet use and average time spent by users aged 8 to 18

	Total daily usage			
	2004	Among users	1999	Among users
Leisure computer use	54%	1:53	47%	:58
Recreational internet	47	1:41	24	:46
E-mail	25	:18	18	:19
Websites	34	:39	22	:30
Instant messaging	24	:38	—	—

Young people's use of computers in 2004 and 1999

COMPUTER ACTIVITY	2004	1999
Playing games	0:19	0:12
Visiting websites	0:14	0:07
Visiting chat rooms	0:04	0:05
E-mail	0:05	0:04
Instant messaging	0:17	NA
Graphics	0:04	NA
Total computer time	1:02	0:27

SOURCE: "Generation M: Media in the Lives of 8–18 Year-olds," (#7251), The Henry J. Kaiser Family Foundation, March 2005., "Zero to Six: Electronic Media in the Lives of Infants, Toddlers and Preschoolers," (#3378), The Henry J. Kaiser Family Foundation, October 2003.

As expected, computer use grows dramatically as kids grow older but it is interesting to note that even among 8-to-10-year-olds, more than one in five visits websites daily and one in ten IMs.

Computer use by age

MEDIUM	8- to-18-year-olds	8- to-10-year-olds	11- to-14-year-olds	15- to-18-year-olds
A. Average daily time with each computer activity				
Games	0:19	0:20	0:17	0:19
Web sites	0:14	0:08	0:13	0:19
Chat rooms	0:04	0:03	0:04	0:03
E-mail	0:05	0:02	0:05	0:06
Instant messaging program	0:17	0:03	0:18	0:27
Graphics	0:04	0:02	0:04	0:05
Total computer	1:02	0:37	1:02	1:22

B. Proportion engaging in each activity the previous day

Games	35%	37%	37%	29%
Web sites	34	21	34	45
Chat rooms	10	8	11	9
E-mail	25	11	26	36
Instant messaging program	26	10	26	39
Graphics	12	9	13	14
Any computer use	54	42	55	61

C. Proportion who used a computer more than 1 hour the previous day

Any computer use	28%	18%	26%	37%

SOURCE: "Generation M: Media in the Lives of 8-18 Year-olds," (#7251), The Henry J. Kaiser Family Foundation, March 2005

Media opportunities will no doubt continue to increase for today's kids. At least 40 percent of kids are going online through high-speed or broadband and one in five connect to the internet through a wireless network, according to Roper Reports. It's fair to assume that as wireless increases in the coming months, so will media opportunities.

In fact, media companies and gaming companies are working together to help one another. Media companies need new outlets and gaming companies need more money due to the high costs of game development. Ads in PC games will not be static, either. Rather, the games will reach out to the web and put in new ads at various times. This means that marketers will be able to buy Reach & Frequency media schedules using PC games.

There is little question that today's youngest children will be even more computer and internet savvy than today's tweens. Nearly twice as many children under age 7 live in a home with internet access as live in a home with a newspaper subscription. Nearly half have already used a computer and 18 percent use a computer daily. These numbers go up to 70 percent and 27

Percent of children aged 4 to 6 who:

Have used a computer	70%
Can use a mouse	64
Use a computer w/o parent	56
Have gone to a children's website	30
Use a computer daily	27
Requested a website	20
Sent e-mail with parent's help	17

SOURCE: Advertising Age

percent, respectively when we look at today's 4-to-6-year-olds, according to an article *in Advertising Age.*

The Third Screen

While computer and internet use has literally exploded among kids over the past few years, we believe that a new, even more significant media is about to become a major factor in marketing to the 4i4l—especially among our teen half. Cell phones, now referred to as the "Third Screen," are poised to become a huge medium and therefore huge marketing vehicle. Reportedly almost half of all kids aged 11 and older already have their own cell phones. And, although it took a while longer to become popular in the U.S. than in Europe, text messaging is quickly catching on. We know how hugely popular IMing has become among teens; text messaging has all of the benefits of IMing without the constraints of having to be on your computer.

There were 4.66 billion text messages sent in December 2004—more than twice the number of December 2003. Two-thirds of all mobile subscribers aged 13 to 24 sent a text message in April 2005, according to an article in *Youth Markets Alert.*

Text messaging is bound to continue to grow significantly as mobile service providers are now beginning to offer "all you can use" text messaging for one low monthly fee. Add to that the fact that text messaging is becoming easier to do as phones are now coming equipped with predictive text. Just hit a letter or two and the phone anticipates the rest of the word for you.

And, if that's not going to be exciting enough for marketers to consider, then think about the fact that all phones will have Global Positioning Systems (GPS). So while 911 operators will be able to quickly help cell phone callers in distress, marketers will also be able to target a message or promotion to a cell phone user when that user is in a specific strategic location, like outside of McDonald's.

Just think of all of those teens with the ability to send and receive messages virtually anytime from wherever they are. Now think of the ways marketers might use this for advertising and promotion.

We'll cover this in more detail in the following chapter.

The third screen offers much more than just text. It is on the verge of offering full video and other downloads. New Sprint alliances with Disney and Warner Brothers and a Sesame Workshop agreement with another phone services company certainly suggest interesting downloads of programs, video clips, and so forth to even young mobile phone users. Specifically, Warner will offer mobile video channels, including *Looney Tunes* and *Friends* and other 3–5 minute videos via Sprint, according to *Youth Markets Alert*.

Multitasking

Adding up all of the various media that kids use during the day, including screen, print, audio, and computer, plus interactive video gaming that alone consumes more than an hour a day, gives us an average daily media exposure among kids aged 8 to 18 of over 8.5 hours! This is up more than a full hour over the past five years. It doesn't leave time for much else does it?

The reason behind kids' significant daily use and exposure to media lies behind their ability to multitask. Today's youth frequently use a number of media simultaneously. They'll read while listening to music or watching TV. They'll watch TV and IM a group of friends at the same time. At least a quarter of the time in which kids are involved with media, they are multitasking.

Total media usage

	Total Usage	Multi-tasking	Internet Usage
8-to-10-year-olds	*8:05*	*27%*	*5:52*
11-to-14-year-olds	*8:41*	*25*	*6:33*
15-to-18-year-olds	*8:44*	*25*	*6:31*

SOURCE: "Generation M: Media in the Lives of 8–18 Year-olds," (#7251), The Henry J. Kaiser Family Foundation, March 2005.

It seems to be especially easy for kids to multitask with TV. In fact, recent research by *Packaged Facts* finds that tweens and teens are just plain losing interest in TV especially as they get older. It's not that they don't love TV. They just have other things to do—especially surfing the internet—that make them love TV less. For perspective, while 80 percent of 8-to-14-year-olds say they love TV, the number drops to 60 percent when looking just at the 12-to-14-year-olds. Not only do kids report going online while watching TV, but also while snacking, doing homework, talking on the phone, and/or listening to music. And, as more and more TV ads direct kids to go online for prizes, webisodes, and so forth, you can bet that the simultaneous use of TV and the internet will increase.

One particular concern arising from looking at TV viewership and multitasking, lies in the fact that so much of it occurs because the TV is often used simply as background noise in the home. Four in ten children live in a home where the TV is on in the background, even when no one is watching. Almost six in ten live in homes where the TV is usually on at mealtime. So, while marketers look at all of the rating points that they are buying on TV and think that they are buying all of those impressions to their mom or child consumer, they may, in fact, only be entertaining the family dog!

Multitasking by 8-to-17-year-olds		
	TV &	Internet &
Talk on phone	34%	22%
Listen to music	22	32
TV/Online	17	18
Mags/books	5	1
SOURCE: Media Outlook		

Since being on the internet is obviously more involving, multitasking here is especially geared to music.

Without a doubt, the biggest change in how we market to the kid part of our 4i4l consumer lies in this chapter. Until recently, TV was the end all, be all, of communicating to the youth in America. Why? Kids need stimuli, and up until recently TV was the only medium offering the benefit of sight, sound, and motion. Not anymore.

Not only does the internet and even the cell phone offer the sight, sound, and motion that TV does, but it *also* demands consumer involvement. Unlike TV where kids can passively sit and watch or not, the new media demand that kids become active, involved participants. You've got to click or at least move your mouse!

Think about it. Remember the primary drivers of kids from Chapter 4? **Power, Freedom, Fun,** and **Belonging.** Now ask yourself, is there any medium better suited to filling *every one of* these drivers than the internet? Kids have the *power* to control and see what they want. In fact everything happens as a *result* of something they do. They have *freedom* to do this wherever and whenever. They get the fun (sensations) of colors, sounds, movements, and unlimited variety. And as for *belonging*—it is an online community.

The computer and phone screens are becoming to today's kids what the TV screen became to the Boomers. Today's youth will no longer need to watch TV to see their favorite programs. They can watch their favorites or even new, unique ones on their PC. Nickelodeon is just now expanding its online offerings to teens with new TurboNick. TurboNick will offer 20 hours of new online programming every week, from full-length episodes to small 30-second clips.

Word of Mouth

In a surround-type of media environment, what media is the most important source for giving kids the ideas they are looking for from what to eat, which clothes to wear, which movies and TV shows are hot? TV is still the king, but it is losing some ground especially to what kids term as "other sources." Patterns suggest these "other sources" are word of mouth which is now so much more accessible through IMs, cell phones, e-mail, online boards, and chat rooms. While kids aged 8 to 17 continue to list TV among the top media alternatives with which they spend their free time, it has dropped by 5 percentage points (to 72 percent of kids) over the past two years. Over the same time period, internet has jumped by some 8 percentage points and is cited by 30 percent of kids.

Kids aged 8 to 17: Source of best ideas about selected items

	TV	Total vs. year ago	Other sources	Total vs. year ago
New clothes	*54%*	*-2*	*23%*	*+8*
New music	*38*	*-2*	*15*	*+6*
Where to shop	*31*	*-5*	*17*	*+6*

SOURCE: "The Consensual Kid," Roper Reports, 2004

Moms and Media

According to recent MediaScan reports, Moms spend an average of

Mom's time with media	
Time spent with various media	
TV	56%
Radio	25
Internet	11
Newspaper	4
Magazines	2
SOURCE: MediaScan Fall 2003	

64.32 hours a week, or over 9 hours a day, with media. She spends most of her time with TV, followed by radio.

Consistent with mom being smarter and better educated than ever before and with the fact that she is also busier and more time-starved, it is no surprise that she, too, has turned heavily to a new medium for her product and service information. The internet allows her to get as much information as she wants and needs when she wants and needs it. As shown above, the internet now accounts for 11 percent of her total media time. According to ClickZ Stats Demographics, 90 percent of moms use the internet because it saves time. AOL Digital Marketing services says that 80 percent of today's moms report that, thanks to the internet, they have been able to free up an average of two hours per week by conducting some of their chores and activities online. *ClickZ News* says that 85 percent indicate that being online and being a part of their children's online experiences is an important part of modern-day parenting. Need we say more?

And this might surprise many marketers: It is the *mom* that is increasingly becoming the online expert of the family. One half of moms indicated that they are more tech-savvy then either their husbands or their children and an additional one in four said she was equal to her husband and children in online expertise, according to *ClickZ News*.

According to Digital Marketing Services, moms who go online, spend an average of almost 17 hours a week doing so—more time online than her teen children and about as much time as she spends watching TV.

Moreover, moms trust the internet to give them the information they want. Half of all moms agree that the internet has changed the way they get product information, according to Tessa Wegert in "Tapping the Mom Market." Ninety-six percent of moms feel the web is a reliable source of parenting information (ClickZ Stats Demographics) and more than 40 percent agree that the internet is *the first place* they look for information. The latter point is critical for today's marketers to realize.

Almost one in three moms report shopping more online than before and not surprisingly, moms largely agree that they return to those sites that make it easy to find what they need, according to Wegert.

So, what else are today's mothers doing online? Just about everything!

Especially important for marketers is the amount of research moms do online for trips, products to buy, recipes, and coupons. When mothers shop online they are looking for a deal.

Mom's time online	
E-mail	96%
Plan/research trips	75
Get news/current events	71
Bank/manage finances	68
Research products to buy	67
Get health information	66
Find recipes	63
Search for discounts, coupons	55
Research home improvement projects	35
SOURCE: AOL/ORC study, 2004	

Forty-one percent of online moms buy goods on sale via the internet that they say they wouldn't have bought otherwise. Some 23 percent have used coupons they have found online for local services, 50 percent have used online coupons for groceries, and 43 percent have redeemed online coupons for household goods.

Another major time consumer for mom—gift shopping—shows signs of quickly becoming a major online task with over three out of every four moms reporting they do this now or would like to do this on the internet according to *ClickZ News*.

Where can we find moms most online? They are all over Yahoo!, AOL, MSN and, because they tend to plan family travel, Mapquest. And, they are on in a big way.

Considering moms' use of the internet, viral marketing or word of mouth may be particularly potent media vehicles to reach them. According to the *BMS Media Study*, word of mouth is the strongest form of marketing among moms. Sixty-four percent say they rely on others' recommendations when buying products for their children and a lot of this word of mouth occurs via e-mail and chat.

Unique monthly visitors: Moms	
Property	Unique Visitors (000s)
Yahoo!	19,193
Yahoo Search	10,626
Yahoo Mail	10,289
Yahoo News	4,551
Yahoo Music	3,662
MSN	15,619
MSN Search	8,283
MSNBC	5,190
MSN Entertainment	4,307
AOL	13,571
AOL Search	5,458
AOL Entertainment	5,444
AIM	4,545
Mapquest	8,302
SOURCE: Media Metrix, June 2005	

As with children, the addition of this new media has not particularly caused moms' use of any other media to significantly decline. They just use *more media!* Fewer than 20 percent of moms feel that they now spend less time with TV and only 13 percent feel they read fewer magazines because of the internet. Radio, the medium that tends to go best with internet usage, has reportedly held about steady, with only about 5 percent of moms feeling that they listen to this medium less because of internet usage.

In general, however, mom just doesn't have the time to merely take it easy and consume media. Rather she must try to fit it in small and generally infrequent time periods. She is among the least likely to view TV, averaging about half the hours an average TV viewer sees in a week, according to AC Nielsen. Like their children, moms multitask with media as well. Almost two out of three (64 percent) of today's mothers report usually doing something else *while* watching TV.

One of mom's favorite things to do when she does have some free time is to read magazines. In a September 2003 Silver Stork Panel, moms said that when they did find extra hours to be by themselves, more than one in three would want to first read a magazine or book, then take a nap. And consistent with this, the Spring 2005 MRI study found that moms are, in fact, 19 percent more likely to be heavy magazine readers than women in general.

Importantly, again, considering moms' heavy schedules, magazines can be ideal vehicles for today's advertisers. Magazines are, by nature, the ultimate opt-in medium. Because they are quick, easy reads and are both entertaining and informative, magazines are ideally suited to moms' hectic moment-to-moment schedules. And unlike TV or radio, reading is not a passive activity. Rather it requires involvement and direct attention and focus. So, if your advertising is attention getting and relevant to moms, this same involvement, attention, and focus can easily be shifted to your ad within the magazine.

Further, of all the media, magazines might be the only ones that moms actually consume, at least in part, *for the advertising*. For perspective, a recent Starcom study found that when readers were asked to pull ten pages that best demonstrate the essence of their favorite magazine, three out of ten of the pages pulled were ads.

Roper ASW, 2005, reports 48 percent of moms believe advertising actually adds to the enjoyment of reading magazines and 71 percent find advertising in magazines to be acceptable versus only 44 percent on TV and 11 percent online.

Moms also find magazines to be the most trusted media. And because of this, and since moms believe that childcare decisions have critical implications, magazines are reportedly their favorite media source for child-rearing advice.

As expected, our 4i4l mom is very likely to read publications, especially regarding childcare. For example, almost one in five moms with kids aged 12 and under read *American Baby*, and 79 percent of all readers of that magazine are moms with kids under age 12.

And, moms certainly have more on their minds than just mothering so various magazines pertaining to general interest, entertainment fashion and style also are favored.

Moms' magazine readership for childcare	Percent of moms w/kids 12 and under	Percent of Readers
Parents	32%	75%
American Baby	19	79
Parenting	19	73
Family Fun	16	73
Baby Talk	15	75
Child	10	76

SOURCE: Simmons, 2004

Knowing these readership trends allows you to consider a broader range of magazines as potential advertising vehicles. While, certainly not as efficient as using childcare magazines, they still reach a significant percentage of the target. Since they are general, you will be paying for a significant amount of readership outside your specific target, but also, since they are general, you might find significantly less direct competition in them, which, in turn will give your brand a better chance to stand out.

Moms' magazine readership for general interest, entertainment, fashion and style		
	Percent of moms w/kids 12 and under	Percent of Readers
People	43%	40%
Family Circle	28	35
Glamour	21	53
Cosmo	18	47
In Style	11	53
Self	9	51
SOURCE: Simmons, 2004		

For example, the president of our Evenflo client directed us to place an ad for a new toddler car seat in *People* Magazine. Since this is extremely expensive, and the client's overall media budget was relatively tight, we encouraged him to stay focused in the general, less-expensive, better-targeted childcare publications. He overruled our direction and so we did place an ad in *People*. Were we wrong! This one ad was credited with moving tens of thousands of car seats in one week! How? It had no competition in the magazine. In a sense it was so unexpected it grabbed attention. The message was right on target and enough of the target consumer was present. Further, since the particular magazine was also perceived as being special to the average retail buyer in this category, some of the retailers bought and displayed extra inventory. We never stop learning!

Also, largely due to her need to multitask, mom is likely to almost always have the radio on. Sixty percent of moms tell us that they listen to the radio every day, according to Wegert. She likes radio and she has many hours and places in which she can access it. Mom spends a lot of time shuttling her kids to school, day-care, after-school programs, and is often out with her kids or on her own to shop. Married women with children spend over an hour a day driving. And, during these times, she is likely to have the radio on.

Another relatively new medium that is having an impact on

today's moms is the emergence of movie-theatre advertising—and it is being noticed! Almost half of our moms agree that they notice lobby and cinema ads, according to Simmons data.

What Part (Child or Mom) of Your 4i4l Consumer Do You Intercept?

Now that we have an understanding of what media our 4i4l consumer is exposed to, it's time to consider various media strategies. How do we reach both parts of our consumer—the child and the mom?

Since the child is so influential in our purchase decisions, doesn't it stand to reason that we advertise directly to the child? Yes, as long as the child is aged 4 or older (as explained in Chapter 3). This is especially true with products and services handcuffed by limited advertising budgets.

Not only is it effective to advertise many of our products and services directly to the child but also it is much more efficient. In almost every case where the child part of our 4i4l is at least 4 years of age, we recommend allocating your media budget *first* to the child and then, if enough funds exist, beginning to build awareness among moms through advertising.

We have found that building effective, motivating awareness among moms by advertising directly to children costs *only one third* of what it might cost if you were to advertise directly to moms. Here's how:

- TV advertising cost per point for women aged 25 to 54 is roughly three times that of the cost per point to advertise to children aged 2 to 11.

- Only about one-half of the women aged 25 to 54 are moms, so half of this money is wasted.

- Therefore, double your cost per point!

- Studies that we have conducted with ASI research show that 33 to 70 percent of children pass along advertising messages to their moms.

- Assume a mid-point of a 50 percent pass-along rate and you have merely doubled the cost of a kid's rating point.

Now do the math!

What type of message would you think has more impact on mom—a passive TV or print ad, or the most powerful "word of mouth" imaginable, her child? And remember what you learned in Chapter 5: A child request actually trumped a mom-observed ad by almost three to one when it came to the reason for buying a specific item.

Naturally, once enough media has been placed against the kid part of our 4i4l consumer, you can go for increased awareness and interest on the part of the mom by going directly to her. Specifically, media studies have shown that media levels of about $7MM are more than enough to saturate the child part of your consumer. And a campaign with as little as 700 TRPs* can hit the peak in reach. Once this has been reached, it is advisable to go for a complementary effort against moms, providing of course, that a mom-appropriate message is developed. (See next chapter for creative solutions).

As Maria Bailey, author of *Marketing to Moms*, states: "All mothers want to please their children. By being unresponsive to advertising messages, a mother risks alienating her child by rejecting the latest "in" products. The fear of creating a playground outcast or teen loner because of the absence of the latest acceptable fashion logo is too great a burden for a mother to bear."

There is another reason to add a mom element to our media plan against the 4i4l consumer. As explained in Chapter 4, not all moms are totally permissive or responsive to their children's input. Rather they need their own reasons and reassurances before purchasing various items. Excellent examples of this can be seen in the campaigns of:

Kraft Mac 'n Cheese. Advertising to children tells them of the fun "cheesy" flavor of mac 'n cheese while separate messages to

---

* TRP = Target Rating Points. This is the total of percent of reach times the average frequency of an ad is seen by the target audience. For example, 150 TRPs could be that 50 percent of kids aged 2 to 11 saw an ad an average of 3 times (50 x 3 = 150).

moms tell them how their children will love the product and that it has wholesome calcium in it (nurturing and health).

McDonald's. McDonald's uses several messages to kids such as various prizes in Happy Meals, and more. To moms, McDonald's separately sends the message that the Chicken Nuggets now are made of all white meat (health).

One important exception to our kid-first rule is advertising to our 4i4l is for those product or services that have far more mom benefits than child benefits. For example, mom should be first if the primary purpose of the product is health or medicinal. Even in these cases, however, remember to do something to let mom know that you are also doing your part in helping her to make her child more receptive, like offering a kid friendly package or addressing her child in separate advertising.

Juicy-Juice. has long advertised only to moms, but their primary claim and reason for being is the fact that the product is made of 100 percent juice—a claim that kids don't care about!

Many times companies are faced with products or services that are considered to be "all family." There are many products that truly are *consumed* not by just mom or her child, but rather, by just about everyone in the family. How does our 4i4l consumer play an important role here?

As with any product or service consumed by more than just one individual, the true objective of the marketer must be to determine the most efficient and effective way in which to get that product *into* the *house*. Once it is in the house, it is there for everyone in the family to consume.

So, here too, if it is your objective to get the mom of the house to bring your particular "all-family" product into the home, then we believe that the rules of the 4i4l consumer again take over. That is, if there is a solid kid benefit, then first for efficiency and impact, target media towards the kid part of the 4i4l; then go to mom. Just remember the influence our kids have over family products as observed in Chapter 5.

How Do You Intercept?

Once you have decided which part of the 4i4l consumer you are going to reach you can craft the best media plan for accomplishing this.

You can try to reach both the child and the mom simultaneously, but this is generally quite expensive. In addition, creatively, you must ask if a more specific creative message to each might work even better. However, assuming you have developed an ad that you believe can work well against both your kid and mom parts of our 4i4l, then your two best choices are:

TV. The largest-reach vehicle is still TV but to effectively generate simultaneous awareness of both child and mom generally requires expensive, highly rated prime-time programming. This is usually far more expensive then executing separate kid and mom campaigns.

Radio. Half of all radio listening occurs while in a car. And many times it occurs with both mom and child in the car. One particular radio channel, Radio Disney, has done a nice job capitalizing on this realizing that, as with most other things, mom wants to please her children so she is open to listening to a children's radio station when driving with her children in the car.

In intercepting your kid part of our 4i4l, you must, if possible start with TV. It is still the dominant part of kids' daily media consumption, at over three hours a day among 8-to-14-year-olds and 2.5 hours among teens. It is also multi-sensual, employing the sights, sounds, and actions that today's kids require. It is generally efficient to buy, especially for kids and tweens because you can target just a few key cable networks like Nick, Cartoon, WB and reach about 84 percent of the target audience.

It is extremely important to use a multimedia approach when possible. Today's kids (and moms) are much more in control of their

Banners

Traditional	A static graphic delivered on a web page. When clicked, it takes you to a single URL.
Interruptive	A banner which has elements that move either with or without user interaction. This can include full motion video with audio. This kind of banner can have elements that animate over the page if you use a technology like PointRoll.

Viral — Creating humorous or engaging videos, games or animations that motivate the user to pass it on based on the content.

AOL/KOL

Main Page Sponsorship	Sold by week, sponsoring the entire "home page" of the main page of KOL.
Virtual Product Placement	Attaching your name to a feature of KOL (search engine, navigation, etc.)

AIM

Buddy Video	Embedding video at the top of the buddy list of AIM.
Out of Banner	A banner at the top of the buddy list that has an element that will "fly" out of the banner, over the desktop then return to the banner. It can leave a message behind.
Expressions	A "skin" which affects the look of the Buddy List. It can also have an interactive game in the side bar. When a user chats with another user the user can see and load the expression from her chat window very easily making this have the potential of being very viral.

Multi-World — Using a "real world" execution that has an online element, such as giving out codes to be redeemed online. An example of this would be the Pepsi iTunes giveaway.

Landing Page — Sometimes an online marketing program requires a special fulfillment page, separate and different than the home page of the client. This may contain additional information, incentive redemption, or registration. That is referred to as a landing page.

media through TiVo, and so forth. They multimedia task often, and many times TV serves solely as a background medium.

Adding an aggressive internet element is especially important. Remember, the average kid user of the internet uses it almost one-and-a-quarter hours daily! You can choose to encourage kids to go to a corporate site which might offer more involvement with the brand, or at least, run advertising online. There are so many ways in which to use the internet, from simple banners to including a video on the top of one's buddy list, to sponsoring a home page in the main page of KOL (Kids On Line, part of America On Line). Here is a quick rundown of available options that now exist.

Just to make planning your interactive effort a bit easier, we have included our online Marketing Pyramid, developed by WonderGroup's Director of Interactive, Jeff Jones.

Online Marketing Pyramid

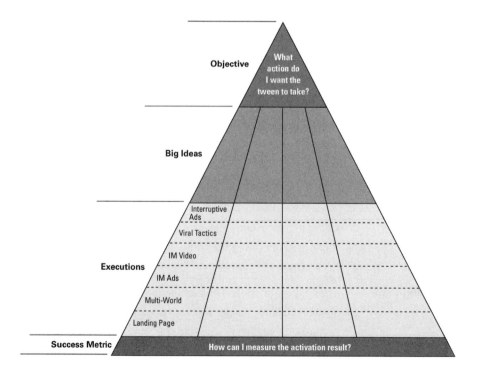

Lastly, magazines, while used for only a small part of the day, are still an inexpensive way to target the kids' segment and, what is becoming important in today's multimedia tasking era, magazines are a medium that *requires* their users to be involved with them. So, unlike TV or radio that can be tuned out by the consumer, magazines are an all or nothing. A few select magazines like *Nickelodeon*, *Sports Illustrated for Kids*, and *Disney* will reach as many as 46 percent of today's kids.

Teens, on the Other Hand

Teens are one of the hardest segments to reach efficiently. They watch less TV than other kid segments, and they are far more mobile and on the go. It doesn't mean you should avoid TV targeted to teens with such networks as MTV and WB, or particularly highly rated shows like *The OC*, but watch the cost. What it does mean is that media other than TV becomes even more essential. Radio use increases sizably with this group, so by all means, add this to your media mix. Targeted print is an option as well. Several studies confirm that teens actually *look* for ads in their magazines, especially since they are reading their magazines to help them to know what is in and what is not.

Word-of-mouth groups, aka buzz marketing, have also surfaced as a marketing tool to this age group. In these cases, companies employ word-of-mouth specialists to spread news to teens concerning their products or services. At least one such company, Tremor, claims to have identified teens that are especially prone to spreading news to other teens, so it targets its clients' news to these "news-spreaders" or "connectors." This type of effort tends to be especially useful for those products and services that teens like to talk about, such as music and entertainment.

Another creative way in which companies now try to intercept teens is through product placements in virtually all kinds of entertainment from movies to videogames to song lyrics. For example, McDonald's is trying to take advantage of product placement by planning to pay the rap artist 50 Cent every time his song mentioning the company's name is played on the air.

As for mom, we have already made it clear that she is extraordinarily time-starved and her ability to actually give her full attention to media is slim at best. While she too watches TV, it is likely to be as a background to other things that she is doing. Many moms report only being able to actually *watch* TV after 9 p.m., when their kids are asleep. Like her child, she will multitask, so it is important to look at various media elements in trying to reach her as well.

If you can afford it, TV is still a primary medium for reaching her, but a well-targeted magazine effort can do so as well. Almost one in four moms tell us that she enjoys reading magazine ads. Another very creative way in which to efficiently reach mom is through a Free Standing Insert (FSI) in Sunday papers. Generally considered to be a promotional element due to the fact that moms generally go to this section for coupons, it nonetheless is an excellent way to inexpensively make mom aware of your product or service. In a test we conducted with one of our clients we naturally saw mom awareness increase when we advertised to kids via TV. But, interestingly, when we did *nothing but* drop an FSI to moms, her awareness spiked as high as if we were running kid advertising.

Considering that 60 percent of moms listen to radio every day, you cannot ignore this medium, especially for local efforts or short-duration promotional efforts. Radio's ability to target by specific day and week and by specific local area gives it a powerful reason for consideration.

Last, but perhaps most important, you must also be aggressive on the internet. Remember, it is becoming the most useful, dominant media for today's time-starved, information-seeking moms. In fact, a Fall 2002 MediaMark study among young adults (GenY and GenX) revealed that you could reach as much as 72 percent of them weekly on the internet—the same number as can be reached via cable TV!

There are several options you can consider for intercepting our mom online.

First, there are several web-ready marketing tools such as banners, direct e-mail, and advertising on select sites. Advertising on other pertinent sites makes tremendous sense as well. However, in realizing that the main reason moms are going to the internet is to save time, your ads will have to be creative and relevant for mom to take the time to interact with them. An example of such a campaign involves one that ran for the Cincinnati Zoo. Here, the insight is that moms often go to the local city web page to see what is happening in the news in and around the city. So a zoo trivia test and a video of the TV spot that is currently running on TV is placed prominently on one of the key pages. Results have been extraordinary. Click-through rates were reportedly 15 percent on the banner ads, 16 percent on the quiz, and a remarkable 23 percent on the actual video (which was just like an ad).

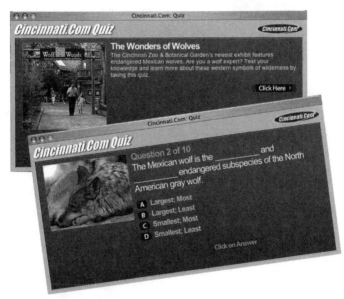

Second, but becoming increasingly important, is a dedicated company or brand site. A dedicated site allows marketers to maintain an ongoing relationship with their consumers and allows consumers to form a stronger relationship with the company or brand. And recall, today's mom will likely look online for her information before making many purchases, so she will be looking for *your site*. A dedicated site also, at times, allows marketers to sell directly to the consumer.

While these are all significant plusses for developing a dedicated site, you must remember that a significant number of dollars and amount of effort will also be needed to attract moms to the site, maintain and engage them, manage the customer relationship online, and determine the return on investment versus other marketing efforts. Nonetheless, considering that moms are increasing their reliance on this type of media, the investment makes sense. A well-placed internet campaign linking to mom's most-visited sites and inviting them to visit your website can be extraordinarily effective. On the other hand, considering that today's moms like to *seek* information and seek more control over their environment, it is no wonder that e-mail campaigns, unless specifically requested, are disliked. Simmons reports that only 17 percent of GenX moms say that they like to learn about products or services via e-mail.

An interesting study of pregnant women conducted by Silver Stork in May 2001, sheds even further light on the importance of non-TV media. Specifically, when asked which media sources these soon-to-be moms found most useful: 90 percent said websites, 81 percent said magazines, and only 17 percent said TV.

Implications: marketers can win her by

- Executing more multimedia promotions or messages for children as well as moms especially considering that TV is becoming more of a "background" media.

- Taking advantage of today's multimedia/multitasking environment by coupling media, that is, requesting internet action within a TV or radio spot or in print.

- Making sure that you have a very easy internet site for moms to find and use for getting information on your product or service.

- Realizing that your TV ads must be even more creative and entertaining if you are to hope to capture the attention of today's multitasking moms.

- Considering where moms go online—planning and researching trips, getting health information, seeking recipes and home improvement information—indicates some interesting media opportunities for today's marketers.

11

Rules of Engagement— How to Communicate

NOW THAT WE HAVE INTERCEPTED our 4i4l, how do we engage it with good solid creative? Just what are the rules of good creative? Well, sorry, we have to chuckle a bit about this question because in the pure sense, creativity can't really have rules or it wouldn't be creative would it? That said, there are some patterns and some "cautions" that we can certainly advise about, and that is exactly what we will do in this chapter.

In our last chapter, we established that there will be many times in which the best way to ensure that your product or service is most efficiently and effectively brought to the attention of our 4i4l is through communicating directly with the child. This way, not only can a child make mom aware of the item, but mom will also have a better understanding as to her child's pre-disposition to consume it, once she spends her time and money to purchase it.

Engaging the Child

While you might think that advertising to kids is a relatively easy task, we have, in fact, found it to be more difficult to do successfully than you would first believe. First of all, according to Nielsen Media, the average child now sees 40,000 TV ads a year, so how are you going to make sure kids see and remember *your* ad in particular?

Virtually all marketers and advertising agencies *think* that they want to do kids' advertising and they *think* it's easy to do. After all, just like having kids themselves, advertising to kids gives them permission to act like a child and have fun. And, inarguably, we've all been kids so we know what it's like to be one. Right? WRONG!

Marketers and their ad agencies can only *act* like a child and not actually *think* like one because, as you saw in Chapter 7 brain development and experiences determine how we think and understand. As you grow older, you can't help but see the world differently than kids do. Unless trained in understanding how children of different ages process information, advertisers are very likely to confuse kids rather than to effectively communicate to them.

Your real-life experiences and your education set you up to understand what is and is not funny. You know what a pun is, an exaggeration, a dream-state, a jump in time, a flash back, and a real-life situation versus a fantasy. It is pre-knowledge that lets you understand jokes! Just go to any young child and tell them a joke such as: "Why did the butter jump out of the window? To be a butterfly!" We guarantee that that child will just about roll on the floor with laughter and then *he* will proceed to give you a joke back, such as, "Why did the toaster jump out of the window?" And when you ask why, he'll say, "to be a toaster fly!" You see, a simple joke that you as an adult *think* that children will understand, still goes over their heads! Hey, try a knock-knock joke on a young child if you really want to be entertained!

In fact, a long-time argument by those not understanding why marketers should advertise to children is that they believe that young children can't tell the difference between an ad and a show. Many times **they are right**. Too many times we have watched kids aged 6 or younger watch what we know to be an ad for them, only to find in research that they thought it was a funny story! That's a BIG problem. We don't know of any marketers who would willingly want to place a substantial amount of expensive media behind an ad that they paid their agency big bucks to create, only to have an ad that merely serves as children's entertainment.

With careful steps, marketers can be more assured that they will in fact, *advertise to* and not just *entertain* the kid part of our 4i4l.

Tips for engaging younger children (aged 7 and under)

Recognition. This is especially critical in communicating to younger children. The role of advertising to younger children is first, and foremost to help them to *recognize* your product or service. Younger chil-

dren cannot understand brands, attributes, and benefits. They can't remember them either. What they do remember and recognize are things that are important to them like characters, jingles, certain package looks. That's why today's leading cereal marketers use characters in their ads and prominently show those characters on their packages. Is Capt'n Crunch a brand or a character? To a child it's *both*. Do kids point to Kellogg's Frosted Flakes, or to Tony the Tiger? To Tony! The traditional thinking of merely showing the product and mentioning a brand's name a few times in a TV ad just doesn't work with younger children.

One brand whose name is particularly hard for kids to understand or remember is one we have mentioned before—Kid Cuisine. Yet, this brand is by far the number-one frozen dinner for kids under age 8. How do they do it? By prominently featuring a character, the penguin named "Kid Cuisine," in every ad and also, clearly showing the blue package on which he is found. Not only do young kids point to him, or recognize him when mom asks her child to pick out a dinner for themselves, but parents of one 3year-old told us that their little girl always asks them to buy the "blue box with the bird on it!" Mom knew what her girl wanted so she bought it.

As you can imagine, it is particularly challenging to make sure that young children recognize what you want them to in your ad (like your brand or package or character) and it is especially challenging trying to ensure that children provide enough information for their parents to understand their request. One disappointing situation occurred recently when we observed a child who we think was about age 3, pointing from her shopping cart and saying "Mac and cheese, mac and cheese." She was clearly pointing to a Kid Cuisine package of mac and cheese. But her mom noticed a less expensive brand of mac and cheese nearby and tried to put that brand in the cart for her daughter. Her daughter continued to cry, "No, mac and cheese, mac and cheese," trying to communicate to her mom that she wanted Kid Cuisine. Mom, being very confused, finally cut the discussion and said, "I got you mac and cheese. Let's go," whereby her daughter just gave up and pouted. We bet that little girl won't eat that mac and cheese either.

Communicate through story line. "What's the story?" What a great question to ask yourself after looking at a proposed TV ad for a product targeted to younger children. As discussed

in Chapter 7, children tend to remember by story, so many times it is advantageous to incorporate a story line into your ad. Not only will a story line aid a child in remembering your ad, but it can also help to make it much simpler for her to follow and comprehend versus an ad with a series of disconnected scenes and statements. A good story has a simple beginning, middle, and end.

But, make certain that the story focuses on the product. Otherwise, again, you might find yourself with an ad that does a great job of merely entertaining your intended audience. If a child is going to remember our story we want her to remember our product with it. Here too, we'll use another Kid Cuisine ad as an example.

Notice the simple story line in the ad at right. Specifically, a child is likely to remember that: "A brother and sister came home with mom after playing sports. Their mom knew what they wanted for dinner, and then Kid Cuisine jumped out of their refrigerator to give them Kid Cuisine All Star Chicken Nuggets which they all sat down to eat and enjoy." A beginning, a middle, an end, and it focused around the product.

Capitalize on repetition. There is much data showing that young children will usually pay closer attention to an ad the second time they see it. In fact, many commercial tests rely on at least a double exposure to an ad before questioning the child. In a presentation to an SRI Marketing to Kids conference, Dr. Langbourne Rust gave this example:

> The first time a young child sees Wile E. Coyote drag the catapult to the edge of the overlook, she will pay only a little attention to it because she has no way of knowing or anticipating what might happen next. But the second time the cartoon is seen, the response is entirely different, the kid is on the edge of her seat, fit to bust with the excitement of knowing what is just about to happen.

Unlike adults, who, after being exposed to an ad will likely screen it out when they see it begin again, a young child will welcome it.

ConAgra
"All-Star w/Robots tag"
:30
3/2005

MOM AND KIDS ENTER FRONT DOOR.
Mom: You guys must be starving!
Girl: I know what I want.

MUSIC/LIGHTS DRAW KIDS TO KITCHEN.
PA Announcer: Wwwwwelcome
back...

LOGO APPEARS ON FRIDGE.
...the World Champion of fun...

KID CUISINE BURSTS THROUGH FRIDGE.
...Kid Cuisine!!

BASKETBALL SPINS INTO PACKAGE.
Kid Cuisine VO: Let's keep the fun going
with my Kid Cuisine All Star Chicken
Nuggets meal made with white meat...

BOY EATS A CHICKEN NUGGET.
Boy: For a taste that can't be beat!

BEAUTY SHOT OF MAC 'N CHEESE.
Kid Cuisine VO:...and my mac 'n
cheese...

GIRL ENJOYS MAC 'N CHEESE.
...is outta here!

BOY FROSTS THE BROWNIE.
Call your shot and frost the brownie.

MOM ENTERS KITCHEN.
Mom: Guys, who's paying for all the
lights?

KID CUISINE POINTS TO HIS BILL.
Kid Cuisine: Uh...you can put it on
my bill...

WONDERBOT LIFTS BOXES AND
ROBOTS LOGO.
Kid Cuisine: Look for my new 'Robots-The
Movie' Meals. From Kid Cuisine!

*Be certain that the child will remember your story when you want her
to remember your product by focusing the story on the product*

Be literal. As pointed out previously in this book, younger children are concrete thinkers and we cannot expect them to be able to rationalize or deduce one thing from another. Unless he or she is well grounded in the taste of your particular type of food, like pizza or fruit snacks (kids do assume all of these taste good), do not expect a young child to understand that *your* particular food product tastes good. You *must* tell them or show them that it does.

However, be careful. Young kids are so literal that what they see is what they expect. And, they see very, very well! They can notice only one thing at a time and cannot make rational decisions, so if you show a particular flavor or color of an item, it better be something acceptable to your audience. If your ad shows a candy in only one color, let's say green, do not expect a child to even guess whether it comes in any other color or flavor, even though you actually do offer several flavors and colors. And if her favorite flavor is strawberry . . . YOU LOSE! Make sure your audience knows this and sees this. Do *not* hope to communicate this abstractly by mentioning that your candy is "available in different flavors," (What's a "different" flavor?).

Tell or show them what to do! A very important part of being literal to younger children is making sure that your ad clearly communicates to the child exactly what it is you want them to do and how to do it. Kids have a natural desire to learn and therefore, they use commercials to teach themselves. Ever watch a young child watch a commercial? They are glued to it, taking it all in. If it clearly shows them what to do, they get it! One particular example that fascinated me was to show a very fast moving, jingle ridden TV spot concerning a game to a 5-year-old. She watched as the spot quickly showed her how kids basically played (and loved) the game. After just one viewing, she understood it entirely (even a detail that the adults missed) just by the visuals.

Studies have shown that preschoolers consistently pay close attention whenever an ad involves show-and-tell. This is especially helpful to them in learning names. To children, name learning becomes a key developmental task. They are hungry to learn names of everything; they want to know what everything is called, and parents seem eager to help them to do this. This learning is then reinforced when the child goes to the store with his or her mom. Stores are full of objects they have seen on TV and as parents and children browse around they spend some time identifying the things around them.

Kids want to know what it is you want of them! If you want a child to use something, then show them that other children like them use it. If you want a child to ask their mom for something, then show them, or creatively tell them to ask mom. It sure makes it easier. It is only after kids get enough experience with advertising and their own power to influence, that they know to simply request something they see in an ad.

Tips for engaging tweens (8–12)

As we saw in Chapter 7, tweens are able to process information better than younger children. They have more experience and pre-knowledge and thus, get more jokes, word plays, time-sequences, and so forth. **But they are still somewhat limited in their ability to fully understand the nuances of advertising.** They are just beginning to be able to be abstract in their thinking. Be careful. They are not adults!

At a recent family get-together, Abbey, a very smart 11-year-old wanted to show me her new favorite website. She said it was called "Millsbury" and she learned about it from her girl friends in school. I asked her if there was any advertising or messages on it and she just shrugged her shoulders and said no. We then went to her room where she quickly and easily logged on.

"Millsbury" turns out to be a General Mills site. It is a fun place where kids can become a character in the city, play games, earn play money, and buy goods and services for their character to live and grow with. As she said, "See, I can buy milk, yogurt, pineapples, *Go-GURT, Trix*. I can play games. I can be a turtle, a frog, girl, *the Trix rabbit, Lucky the Leprechaun. . . ."* She saw *no difference* between General Mills' characters and others. Sure she recognized them (and that certainly has some value to General Mills), but she had no idea what to do about it and when I asked her if she would like to buy these items for real, she wrinkled her nose and said no.

So our advice here is:

Employ many of the same rules as for the younger children. Since tweens are better but far from perfect in their information processing skills, it would certainly not hurt to follow many of the rules mentioned above for younger kids, in ads for tweens. PLUS:

Watch your Age! A key differentiator of tweens from younger kids is that tweens must not think that you are treating them as "babies" or younger children. Talent and action in your ads as well as the storyline (if used), the music, and the situation must be appropriate for kids about age 12. (Remember tweens don't want to think of themselves as younger than they are; age up in your talent *not down*).

Know your friends. Another important difference between tweens and younger children is peer pressure. Tweens need to be sure that their friends do not consider them outsiders. Therefore, when possible, advertising for tweens needs to show or indicate probable peer approval. Note how many ads involving tweens show several "friends" in them together.

Provide opportunity for interactivity. According to David Walsh, educational psychologist of the National Institute on Media and the Family, teachers and school psychologists notice that more kids than ever have trouble sitting still and "It's become harder over the last 10 years to keep kids' attention." Passive creative that requires kids to just sit still and watch or read, will have a difficult time in keeping them involved with your message. Asking them to click onto the internet, or do something else and providing them with multi-sensory stimuli, colors, graphics, sounds, will all become more important. In 2003, Yankelovich found that almost one in three 9-to-17-year-olds reported going online to vote for their favorite things and almost one in five go online to enter contests or sweepstakes. And now these numbers have to be up significantly. Just think of *American Idol!*

Keep your message relatively simple. Costs of advertising sometimes lead marketers to try to get more out of a single ad and as a result try to stick too many messages in one execution. One particularly favorite way is through the use of "tags"—a separate, few-second "thought" added at the end of a TV or radio spot. Generally, they are added to previously aired commercials and therein lies the big problem. According to Ipsos-ASI, advertising builds quickly to kids, leveling off by about 750 TRPs. So, adding a tag after the initial ad has already been established means that marketers are hoping to attract and maintain kids attention right through the 25th second. It's just not going to happen if the kids have seen this ad 10 plus times already.

If we are hoping to impart an extra thought through a tag, the whole ad has to be relatively new and, the tag, or extra thought, should be closely related to the rest of the spot. Otherwise, you run the risk of causing confusion to kids. With confusion, you don't know what, if anything, the child will remember.

Our favorite learning on this occurred many years ago. We were doing an ad for a new Super Soaker MDS, a water gun that could squirt in several different directions (MDS = Multi Directional Spray, get it?). At the last minute, our client wanted us to also add a tag for a Super Soaker Bow and Arrow. Although 25 seconds were devoted to the wonders of the Super Soaker MDS, and only 5 seconds were spent at the end of the spot calling attention to the Super Soaker Bow and Arrow, guess what the kids said the spot was about? Yup . . . a Bow and Arrow!

If you need to impart a lot of news, then it must be done in an integrated consistent manner. One particularly successful spot involved having to communicate a new promotion behind an existing line of meals. We had to show kids how great the meals tasted, plus the fun of the promotion, plus how to enter a contest, plus the prize (which was featured in the last few seconds). Whew! But, because it was all integrated and was presented simply from start to finish, it worked!

Last, if you imply, you die! We can't say this enough; kids of all ages, even tweens, need to know concretely what you are trying to communicate to them. Recently, we tested some print ads from a major retailer trying to advertise to tween girls a new line of accessories available only at their stores. The tween girls tested said it caught their attention and looked like fun, but had no idea what the ad was really communicating. And, when they were asked which store they thought they could find the merchandise they guessed wrong—and the logo of the retailer was in the ad!

Now this doesn't mean you have to be literal and concrete in every instance. Remember, experience teaches, so if a tween already knows and has experience with a category they will have learned from it and will know what it is all about. They *may* already know that a specific new pizza flavored snack probably tastes great because they already know that they love pizza. They know what to do with various clothing, objects, and so forth, so you don't have to literally explain everything to them. *However, to be certain that your audience knows enough about your product or category to not have to use concrete messaging, test your creative first.*

Also, at this age, kids have had plenty of experience with advertising so they do know: that they are seeing an advertisement, to watch it or read it, take in the information, and decide what to do with it (i.e. ask for it, buy it, ignore it).

Can we advertise to all kids, not just older versus younger?

In reality, many times your product or service could appeal to a 4i4l with a child ranging in age from 6 to 12, and it is possible to craft communication to more than one segment of children.

In this situation, it is generally best to consider the primary target of the communication to be a tween because, again, the tween will **not** want to be seen with a product that he perceives as "babyish" in a commercial. Also, while tweens do not want to be perceived as younger, young children **do** want to be perceived as older and will trade up so you would not be alienating the younger child.

However, while considering the primary target of the advertising to be tween, you can still make certain that the overall ad is straight forward enough and simple enough for younger children to understand. Like a well-crafted movie, such as *Shrek,* older kids will appreciate some of the verbal humor, whereas younger ones will understand the visual slapstick humor. Many fruit snack, candy and toy commercials do an excellent job advertising to broader kid audiences.

The Ten Commandments

After reviewing countless hours of kid commercials, we've come up with a summary of our ten commandments for effective ads to kids:

1. *Be mindful of the cognitive development of your ad's target age group.* As we discussed in a previous chapter, kids of different ages think and process information differently. Younger kids operate on a much simpler level than their older counterparts. Your target age group must understand the ad before it can act on it.

2. *Grab your audience's attention early and hold it.* Many kids, especially younger ones, cannot refocus their attention once they've moved it to something else. So if something confuses or bores them in your ad, they "leave" it and cannot mentally come back.

3. *Link your brand to the story.* Kids, especially younger ones, tend to remember things in story form, including ads. Having a brand that is strongly linked to the story told in your ad increases the chances that kids would remember it when cruising the aisles.

4. *Make the brand memorable.* Further building on the theme of brand recall, using mnemonic devices such as jingles and characters (e.g., Kid Cuisine's KC the Penguin and Kellogg's Tony the Tiger) will help kids remember your brand.

5. *Be literal.* As most people with children already know, kids are very literal. What they see and hear is what they get. Therefore,

don't make your messages or claims too vague or abstract. Kids will either misinterpret or not even comprehend the point you're trying to get across. For example, if your product comes in certain flavors, tell the child exactly what those flavors are.

6. *Watch out for distractions.* Kids pay attention to the darndest things, sometimes the wrong things. Younger kids suffer from centration, and will center their thoughts and attention on just one part of your ad or product that stands out to them. It might be the little kitten in the ad; it might be the cute baby; but it might *not* be the product or the message.

7. *Humor, music, and anticipation increase kid involvement.* Kids are all about fun, and nothing says fun more than jokes, tunes, and the element of surprise. Any combination of these can serve as a hook for your ad. But make sure the child understands the joke. If not, he or she will think that *you* are stupid.

8. *Do not pick on living things.* Here is one out of left field. So far we've been talking about "dos," but we felt it necessary to include one "don't." Make sure your ad does *not* show kids picking on other kids or animals. Kids' picking on adults is okay, and cartoon animals picking on each other might be okay, but our research with many commercials found that in general it's better to show the nicer side of kids.

9. *Boys will be boys; girls will be either—but it's best to show both.* Girls respond to either boys or girls in ads, but boys will usually not respond favorably to ads with girls as the only talent. There are a few exceptions to this—for instance if the girl is an athlete. Even with this, however, girls respond better to actually seeing girls in an ad.

10. *Test before committing.* Before committing the big bucks on media, make certain that your audience likes the ad. Likability is still the strongest, most important part of any commercial to a child.

Kids Online

Considering how important interactive media is becoming to kids,
you must also look at how to
engage your kid part of the 4i4l
consumer online as well as by traditional media.

A good website should align
itself with the key kid motivators:
Power, Freedom, Fun, and Belonging. The Kidzworld site is one of
many that does this well.

- **Power** is given by the site immediately asking the user to rate
  its comics. It is implied that the rating given by the kids will
  influence how the site is developed in the future. The chance to
  "win" several prizes is also empowering.

- Joining the blogs or chats provides **belonging**.

- **Fun** comes from the free online games

- **Freedom** is there too. No restrictions on entering any part
  of the site.

Remember, too, that we have heard from psychologists that it is
believed that as a result of the virtual explosion in the amount of
online and video gaming used by today's kids, their minds have probably undergone some form of change. Let's carry this out a bit and
realize that if these same kids are so engrossed in fast-moving, fast-
sounding, and colorful gaming, then your online efforts must follow
suit if you are to keep them engaged.

Let's take a look at some of the ways in which another group is
are now successfully accomplishing this.

A great example of a site that has adapted to this change in how
today's kids process information is *sparktop.org*.

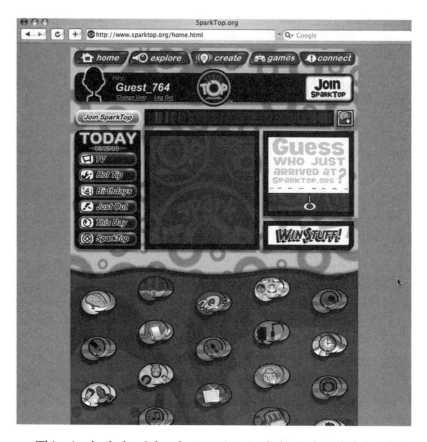

This site built by Schwab Learning is dedicated to helping kids who learn differently, such as kids with dyslexia or ADHD and is an awesome resource to help parents collaborate with their kids on ways to deal with their challenges.

The major categories along the top navigation could not illustrate more clearly an understanding of what motivates kids.

1. **Explore** allows kids to have a sense of freedom.

2. **Create** gives kids the power to express themselves.

3. **Games** allow them to be immersed in an environment of fun.

4. **Connect** allows them to experience the validation and acceptance of their peers.

Kids Are Critical

One additional important point to realize is that today's kids are becoming more critical of advertising. Remember they are much more savvy as consumers compared with previous generations of kids. They have more alternative media outlets than ever before and soon, thanks to TiVo and other options, they will be even more in control of the advertising that they take in. In fact, Roper Report says almost two thirds of kids aged 8 to 17 say they would be very likely to skip commercials if they could.

Therefore, entertainment value is more important than ever in crafting messages to this audience. And, at least currently, advertisers are not doing a great job in this. According to the 2004 Roper *Youth Report,* only 60 percent of kids now agree that commercials are often fun or interesting to watch—a drop of 13 percentage points in the last two years.

Tips for Engaging Mom

Remember, today's moms are on the go some 15 to 16 hours a day. They get up early, and go to sleep late. On rare occasions they have time for a bath or a nap. Now, add to this the fact that today's moms are savvy consumers, well educated, and that they aren't exactly fans of advertising in the first place. Thirty percent of today's moms state that they don't like advertising and 24 percent agree that advertising in general is a waste of time. Thirty-seven percent of today's media-controlling moms say that they will change channels when commercials come on, according to Wegert.

Now, try to get in front of her and engage her with your message. Think it's going to be easy to get her to spend what's left of her valuable free time giving her attention to your message?

Be relevant . . . Be simple!

Too many of today's moms feel that advertisers are not in sync with their needs. More than half of mothers say they often see ads that send moms the wrong message and 30 percent say they see ads that actually offend them. Less than one-quarter think TV or print advertising connects with them, according to the Center for Media Research.

So, what is in sync?

Help her to be a great mom. Throughout this book we have shown how today's moms feel that clearly the most important thing in their lives is to be a great mom. Therefore, it stands to reason that to be most effective, you must package your message in a way that quickly and clearly explains how your product or service will contribute to helping her be such a mom and when appropriate you must also recognize the type of mom she is, that is, permissive or restrictive. Offer a way to feed and nourish her children more easily, a way to balance her life, a method to allow her child to get the best available, help her to help her children learn, or a product to keep her family healthy and so on. Advertising that speaks to moms about bettering the lives of their children, getting them off to an early start, or enriching their experiences can be observed throughout the media. The success of such companies or products as Sylvan, Baby Einstein, and Leap Frog, now the third largest toy company, can attest to this.

Less time alone in the kitchen.

More time together at the table.

Turn dinnertime into quality time with new tools, tips and recipes from Lipton and The Pampered Chef.

Respect her needs. Know and respect her needs. She needs time, so keep it short and simple. Make it easy and convenient to do business with you. Give your company's contact information and URL in your ads to suggest this. Also, show mom how your particular product or service will save her time or money or make her life a little simpler so she can be an even better mom. One ad that does a nice job is the ad WonderGroup created for Lipton Recipe Secrets.

Speak to her life stage. There are times in a mom's life that big things happen regarding her and her children. It can be when she first finds out she's pregnant, when her child becomes a toddler, when her child goes off to school, when her child eats all by himself, anything that can have a major impact on how she feels as a mom. Many products do not rely on a specific life stage of moms, but that does not mean that creative can't be made sharper by targeting a specific message to a certain life stage.

Do not segment by stay at home vs. working mom. Many moms stay at home but also work from home, many work part-time, and many stay-at-home moms work just as hard (if not harder) as those who work outside the home.

Show children. If being a great mom is the most important goal for today's moms, what's a great way to get her attention? Through children! And let's face it, there is no such thing as too much of a good thing. When appropriate, show children in your ads. Moms will immediately know that the message is for her if it shows children the same age as her children. Three-quarters of moms say that ads featuring children in them rank high in effectiveness, according to the Center for Media Research.

That's not to say that placing children in ads, or showing moms in ads are the *only* ways to capture our mom's attention. Otherwise there would be no need for "creativity" from our advertising agencies. In fact, while children do capture mom's hearts and eyes, there are already a tremendous number of ads incorporating kids as the attention getters. Just look at a *Parents* or *American Baby* magazine. Lots of cute ads with children in them, but in many cases, just about *any brand* can be substituted in each ad. So, when you do use children in your ads, do it creatively and try to make them tie into your brand and message.

Again, we'll use an Evenflo ad to show an example of a unique use of children to deliver a specific message to moms, namely that "Evenflo products just seem smarter."

Entertain. Being sensitive toward her valuable time, it is wise to entertain when possible and appropriate. If she is giving you her time, what are you giving her? Moms tell us they prefer humor and engaging storylines whenever possible. Also, you might consider using mass media like TV to deliver an emotional appeal for the brand and relegate the more boring specifics to the internet or another medium like print where women are more likely to go for information-gathering.

Entertainment is especially important when mom is on the internet. Remember, she is primarily using the net to save time and she is in absolute control on what she intends to look at and read with this medium. Because of this, she tends *not* to pay attention to internet ads nearly as much as ads in other media. The Center for Media Research finds that only 6 percent of moms say they pay attention to internet ads compared with 74 percent for TV ads and 62 percent for magazine ads. This does not mean marketers should ignore the internet as an important advertising media. Rather it suggests that marketers must be extra creative with this medium if they hope to engage moms here.

Be visual. Because of mom's experiences growing up with MTV type of graphics, we have learned that ads must be highly visual and get to the point quickly and easily. If she requires more information, give her access to it, again, quickly and easily through the internet, or in a separate sidebar if you run print advertising.

E-mail? Moms use a lot of e-mail. But, in order to engage her, e-mail messages and offers must be simple and to the point. A survey conducted by Lucid Marketing and Email Labs in May 2005 reports that moms are likely to decide whether to open an e-mail based on who the e-mail is from. Subject lines that mention price discounts or other savings are most appealing. But, once they decide to open the e-mail it had better provide easily accessible specifics. Prices and product photos are highly important for them when deciding on whether they will click through to the website. In summary, Lucid warns that a solid e-mail: "Tells her proudly who you are, makes a compelling and relevant offer and above all, shows respect for her precious time."

Websites? With moms looking on the internet for information, websites can be a very important part of your overall marketing commu-

nications **but** they should also be simple and easy for mom to get the information she is looking for. The content should be relevant, offering helpful information and tips, not just product-related information. Dialog between mom and the company and mom-to-mom should be facilitated. And, most of all, the site should be welcoming and friendly. The Huggies site shown on page 177 is just one example of a solid mom-friendly site.

When it comes to being a great mom, mothers today actively seek the recommendations of others, especially when it comes to buying products for their children. The first place where new moms go to find out about products for their children are other, experienced moms. And, she will look for these moms on the internet.

So when communicating to mom on the internet, your message and creative should attempt to capitalize on and promote moms' tendencies to want to spread the news. Add a "Send this Page to a Friend" tool to your site to make it easy for moms to share a good thing when they see it. Include items to make it especially rewarding to share such as a pertinent story, cartoon, joke, or picture. Just make sure your name or sponsorship is clearly a part of it.

12

Exciting Your Consumer

ONE THING THAT WE HAVE seen change over the years is the 4i4l's need and expectations for "news." Maybe it's because so much has changed so often during their short lives. Maybe it's because we have all been spoiled by what the internet and mobile phones and computers have done for us. Maybe it's because retailers, like Wal-Mart, put pressure on suppliers to come up with more and more exclusive, new product offerings. Whatever the reason, if it's not new—BOO!

For any marketer whose 4i4l consumer product category involves a reasonable amount of child influence we say: **Good News**. Kids are always looking for something new, so if you are introducing a new product, kids could be easily drawn to it. **Bad News**. Kids are always looking for something new. So, if you are *not* constantly offering "something" new, bye-bye. Our creative director recently told us that his 9-year-old daughter recommended to her mom that they purchase a certain new flavor of yogurt. After mom bought it, it was quickly consumed. So, her mom bought it again, and again it was consumed. Again, and again it was eaten. Now, after a month of this, he finds a stack of this yogurt, collecting frost in his refrigerator. Why? Something else new came along in yogurt and his daughter wanted that one!

ASI advertising research confirms the need for "news in kid-directed advertising." ASI reports that what makes one commercial score better than others for children is largely the fact that that the ad taught kids something *new*.

We caution many of our clients to look at their marketing plans for the next year and begin with the question, "So, what's new?" If the answer is nothing, then expect some problems because kids will lose interest in your brand. And believe us, your competition will make sure that kids will lose interest in your brand by introducing something new themselves.

What's New?

New can be *anything* that wasn't there before. It can be a new flavor, size, color, or a new promotion (especially with a new package), or even an entirely new product. But remember, today's mom still wants simplicity, so news that just serves to confuse her, like a meaningless package change, will annoy her!

Product News

There is an important difference between simply creating product news behind an already existing brand versus developing an entirely new product. While entirely new products can be more newsworthy and may be necessary for most companies to continue to grow, creating simple product news behind an existing brand may also be an excellent way in which to keep your current brands healthy and alive with the 4i4l. Plus, it is usually much faster and less costly to execute. There are many great examples of this:

- **Capt'n Crunch.** Whether it's "now with blueberries," "smashed berries," "airhead candies," there is always an in-and-out version of this perennial favorite hitting the shelves and being advertised.

- **Go-GURT.** Go-GURT moves its flavors in and out, offering xtreme sours, different colors, different looking packages (like glow in the dark) and more.

- **M&M's.** Flavors and textures like mint, crispy, and now sizes like minis and the new Max all keep this giant brand as new as if it were just born.

- **Hershey Kisses.** Old brand, new excitement for both parts of the 4i4l. New limited-time flavors like caramel, orange cream, and cherry cordial.

- **Kid Cuisine.** Dinosaur-shaped chicken nuggets one month, Shrek-shaped another, bug-shaped another, and so on.

- **Kraft Mac 'n Cheese.** New pasta shapes like wheels, characters, and packages with Sponge Bob on them.

You get the picture, a flavor, a color, a box, a size, or a texture, just to keep the 4i4l looking for "what's new."

Consumer Promotions

The old rule was to use consumer promotions primarily to provide short-term sales lifts, usually through inducing greater trial or increased purchase. But, consumer promotions can also be an excellent way in which to create news and excitement behind your brand. Kids, especially, have proven to be very attuned to on-pack promotional offers, especially if accompanied by a clear, illustration that has impact.

Another reason for using consumer promotions as a way to create news is that they do a nice job of activating your consumer to have a new, hopefully greater, *experience* with a brand. Our studies have shown that the more a consumer experiences a brand in different ways, the more she will become involved with it, bond with it, and become a more loyal consumer.

When promoting to moms, the golden rule is, just as with advertising, be in sync with her needs, especially the need for simplicity and ease. In short, help her to be a great mom!

Promotions that Work Well with 4i4l

Here, as in other parts of our marketing mix, you should use *insights* to help craft your thinking. Hopefully, some of the insights you will develop come from this book. Others you will develop from your own observations and research. Nonetheless, to help you get started, here are a few examples that we know have worked for our clients.

Insight: Mom loves to please her children, so various, kid-directed promotions also have appeal to moms.

Licensed or entertainment-based on-pack promotions. Items featuring a licensed character or movie property tend to work well as moms know what characters their children really like. Put a SpongeBob on your package and moms know their children will love them for bringing it home.

An example of this involves Lipton Chicken Noodle Soup. The Lipton Chicken Noodle Soup brand was looking for some news as a way to revitalize its sales. Lipton Chicken Noodle Soup skews heavily toward a 4i4l whose child is very young, so we developed a pro-

motion involving the PBS show *Clifford the Big Red Dog* (The Big *RED* dog and the little *RED* box!) Clifford was displayed prominently on every box of Lipton Chicken Noodle Soup and a 15 second TV spot for Lipton ran on the *Clifford* PBS show.

The Clifford on-pack promotion enabled Lipton Chicken Noodle Soup to participate in a Wal-Mart retailainment event where the stores built huge doghouses using Lipton Chicken Noodle Soup boxes. For the first time in many years, the brand received end cap displays and floor-stand placement. Its on-shelf presence also improved dramatically and moms bought more boxes!

Insight: Moms are stressed over time and money.

Free product samples go a long way toward attracting moms to try your product. Not surprisingly, it is the first promotion that comes up when we ask moms for their favorite offers.

FSI (free standing insert) coupons are still used by a lot of today's moms. Forty-eight percent of GenX women who read grocery advertising inserts said they regularly use coupons.

Avoid promotions requiring mom to take extra steps. Many moms nix rebates and money-back guarantees because they just don't have the time to take advantage of them.

Insight: Moms value relationships and word of mouth.

Opportunities to join company panels or give advice or just spread the word are welcome and so are loyalty reward programs as long as they don't require too much of a wait to see results (remember time!).

Encourage word of mouth for your promotions by making it easy for moms to do so. For example, use a pad of coupons, where appropriate, so that moms can take you for a friend, too. Always include links or referrals on promotion websites and e-mails.

One particular way in which word of mouth was used, involved Lipton Recipe Secrets (LRS) joining forces with Pampered Chef— a well-respected organization which sells cooking appliances through consultants who host cooking parties. During this promotion, cooking parties were thrown for moms in search of *quick and easy meal solutions* (another time-stressed insight). LRS provided Pampered Chef consultants with free samples for use, and coupons to disseminate during their demonstrations. LRS received top-of-mind awareness among the Pampered Chef consultants and, in turn, these con-

The Pampered Chef celebrates another Fast Family Favorite with Lipton Recipe Secrets.

The secret to a successful Kitchen Show—
a fresh idea that's quick and easy.

sultants became credible word-of-mouth endorsers for the LRS brand. Moms actually got to see and taste the LRS recipes making them true believers.

Insight: Kids love to interact and have power.

Promotions that offer a choice of prizes are intriguing to children. In testing various promotions among tweens, the ones that clearly rose to the top were those offering choices. Think of how exciting it is for a child to not only imagine winning but also imagine what it is he or she would choose.

Promotions offering kids the chance to vote are also big. We had the privilege of developing and fielding a promotion with Kid Cuisine and Cartoon Network where kids could *choose* between a Dexter meal (mind) or a Powerpuff Girls meal (muscle). Then they could also go online and *vote* for their favorite. Results were enormous. Hundreds of thousands of votes were cast. In-store displays and supporting coupons helped drive record sales.

Insight: Boys will be boys; girls will be either, (but they would rather be girls).

Unless there is the opportunity to run parallel promotions for boys and girls (like the Power Puff Girls vs. Dexter promotion discussed above) or unless your brand or service appeals to only one of the sexes, promotions should be gender neutral. Entertainment, electronics, most sports, bedroom décor, travel and for tweens and teens, music, all appeal to both boys and girls. LunchMakers partnered with

Nintendo and its new game Donkey Conga. The promotion was delivered on pack and offered kids a chance to win a GameBoy or PlayStation2 console and the new game. To make the promotion even sweeter, the winners would get two extra sets of prizes to share with their best friends. Remember, tweens love to "belong" so friendship and sharing is key. This promotion was rated as one of the brand's strongest efforts ever.

Insight: Moms want to be a great mom, but also need a little pampering/balancing.

Sweepstakes offering family vacations or prizes that can pamper her such as spa trips, bath products, or house cleaning for a year, for example, can find some strong mom interest.

Insight: Today's mom is more educated and marketing savvy then her predecessor.

Promotions that involve celebrity endorsements are among the lowest of interest except if that endorsement makes a whole lot of sense!

Insight: Your 4i4l lives largely on the internet.

Importantly, heavy internet usage on the part of our 4i4l has opened up brand new, significant, and powerful promotional opportunities— opportunities that fit perfectly with the needs of today's moms for simplicity and of today's kids for instant results. For example, marketers can now offer codes printed on their packages, allowing consumers to enter a special website where they can see if they won a prize. Or, especially fun for kids, codes on packages or in-store materials can give them points for "extra power" when playing specific online games. Think of it. The options of using the internet as part of a consumer promotion can be countless!

New Products

The biggest news generally comes from new products. Time-consuming to develop, costly to introduce, highly risky, but still well worth it when successful!

Over the years, we have come to appreciate that the best opportunities for new product success are based on what we call RAMBO. That's an acronym for Relevant, Appealing, Motivating, Believable and Ownable and that is what the benefit of your new product better offer if it intends to stick around.

Relevant

To make sure a new product idea is relevant to our 4i4l, you must be sure that it is grounded in a firm, true insight. Without a true insight, there is really no need for your new product.

For example, answering an insight like, "Mom is looking for help with her everyday challenges by making her life more simpler," has led to some interesting successes such as: P&G's Swifter, Rubbermaid's Storage Solutions, or Glad's Press and Seal. They have made cleaning, organizing, and storing easier for moms. Or consider insights like, "Mom is looking for help to more easily encourage her children to learn or keep her children entertained," and you *may* come up with Leap Frog's Jump Start products or the many new DVD releases that have surfaced to help mom educate her little ones.

Johnson & Johnson found an insight in watching moms of toddlers bathe their children. The company realized that moms didn't really have the bathing products for toddlers. There were baby products and kid products, but toddlers presented unique cleaning needs to the mom. Products still had to be very gentle but a lot stronger than the available baby products. Their insight, "I wish there were products that could specifically help me make bath-time and the grooming of my toddler easier and help me to teach him basic hygiene habits." This resulted in the recently successful global launch the new Johnson & Johnson Buddies line of personal care products for toddlers.

Appealing

For kids, it comes down to finding new ways in which to satisfy at least one, preferably more, of their primary drivers: Power, Freedom, Fun, and Belonging. Filling these emotional needs is more important than any other brand attribute you may offer. Again, kids are generally on the lookout for something new, so if you build it, they are likely to come, as long as what you develop actually satisfies their drivers.

Ever wonder why such kid products as Go-GURT, LunchMakers, Fruit by the Foot, Gameboy, and other highly successful kids brands became just that? Look at any kid mega brand and you'll see that they fill virtually every one of the major kids drivers.

But remember, your insights must be true!

A while ago we were looking at a new product concept for a food company wishing to introduce a higher-priced, more-nutritious granola bar for kids. And this was based on *what* insight? "My kids love to eat granola bars. I wish there was a granola bar that was nutritious for my kids." Huh? Moms already perceive granola bars as nutritious—nutritious enough that they certainly would not jump at the chance to pay even more money for one with marginally better nutrition. Fortunately, some quick qualitative research helped this company realize its mistake before it spent too many dollars perfecting and launching this item.

And, another caution, just because *you* think you have developed a product that will satisfy a child's driver, like fun, does not mean that it truly will. Kids today are exposed to, and aware of so many new items promising new and better fun, that there is a good chance that your new item might not match up. Or, at the very least, your great new fun item won't be able to sustain the fun for very long once kids see the next new fun item. Remember the Heinz Green Ketchup we talked about in our chapter on insights? Boy was that fun! Kids got to squirt a fun new color of Ketchup on their food. And then Heinz, realizing that they had to keep their product new and fun, launched another color, purple and then another color. And kids said, "Boy that color is fun, and the next is fun and . . . and wait a minute! It's no longer fun coloring my food! I want the next fun food idea!" And boy, they had a lot to choose from!

Motivation

Developing a new product based on a solid consumer insight is just the start of your work, because, as we all know, on the surface, most consumers are already pretty satisfied with the products they have. Plus, while moms may be in need of the help that a new product might offer, they also have a strong aversion to wasting valuable time and money on products that might not perform as promised. Kids have their own roadblocks. Younger children do not like to take chances on things they are unsure of—especially food. Remember the old Mikey commercial: "You try it. No, you try it." That's for real! Tweens and teens have their barricades as well. It is crucial for these kids to feel your new product will not prove risky to their needs of belonging, fitting in, and being cool.

So, is your new product based on a *strong enough* insight, or is it such a *great answer* to a problem that moms or kids or both will be compelled to try the product on their own? Proper concept testing can offer crucial answers here. With these answers you can better determine what incentives or assurances you might have to offer to get 4i4l to move on it.

Believable

Do consumers believe your product can offer the benefit that you say it can? Reasons to believe can come from an emotional connection including imagery, feelings, or sensory information. For example, in Kellogg's recent introduction of Tiger Power, a healthier, whole grain cereal aimed at helping young kids grow healthy and strong, the brand name (based on Tony the Tiger), Tony's identity, and the Kellogg's name all helped make this idea believable for moms.

Reasons to believe can also come from rational, functional points of difference. In the case of Kellogg's Tiger Power, this was presented, as it is the only cereal to provide protein, calcium, and whole grains. Ideally believability should come from both emotional and functional points of difference.

For young kids, reasons to believe tend to be simpler. Does the product seem to be for kids like me? Do I see kids my age using it and liking it? TV and packaging go a long way in providing this assurance to kids.

Ownability

You might have done everything right so far. You have developed a great new product based on a solid response to a well-thought-out insight. Research shows that your consumer believes it can deliver what is promised and she is ready to purchase your product.

The big question now is: "Can you own it?" Is what you are proposing already "owned" by another brand and if so, can you own it too? In the case of the food company that wished to launch a nutritious granola bar, another reason that their insight was not correct was because it was already owned in the category. A nutritious granola bar? Try Quaker Chewy Granola or Kellogg's NutriGrain.

Even if what you are proposing is currently not owned by any other existing brand, is there another brand that can easily take away your ownership?

Once, we launched a new product for Borden Cheese called Big Cheese. The insight was strong. Kids and moms wished for a cheese big enough that it covered the bread with just one slice. Kids loved it because it provided a cheese taste in every single bite of sandwich. Moms loved it because they could give it to their kids without needing to use two separate slices. The Borden name and the actual size of the cheese slice provided believability from both emotional and functional points of difference. Testing of the character on the package and the brand's TV advertising showed motivation would be there. BUT, unfortunately, there was also a company by the name of Kraft! Understandably, it wasn't too keen on letting anyone "own" any part of the cheese market other than itself.

Big Cheese became a very quick success in the marketplace for Borden, that is, until Kraft decided that *it* would own it. Kraft copied the size, dropped its price, and strongly supported its introduction. There was only room for one big slice in the category—and it wasn't Borden. Borden could not protect the uniqueness of Big Cheese and hence it lost its ownership to the more aggressive marketing of the number one brand in the category—Kraft.

In summary, ownability can come from several areas. As with "believability," ownership can come from an emotional point such as the brand's power itself or an appeal to a unique consumer (kids vs. adults). Perhaps, Borden would have been smarter to use its Elsie the Cow icon more strongly in an effort to better own the Big Cheese. Ownership can also come from functional points if you can protect them and no one else can offer them.

13

Some Surprise 4i4l Examples

AS YOU HAVE LEARNED BY NOW, the 4i4l Super Consumer is alive and active in almost every purchase category that affects a family unit in any way. Of course there are exceptions. For example, most serious healthcare issues and financial investment and tax decisions, which are abstract and complex, are areas in which parents make the decisions based solely on their perspective of what is best for the family. But today, many minor or less serious healthcare issues do involve the 4i4l—such as which vitamins, cough drops, toothpaste, or cough medicine to purchase.

Let's spend some time talking about how some of today's most savvy marketers, in categories not usually associated with kid and mom, have adopted a 4i4l approach.

Retail

Retail marketers have historically talked directly to moms. This was the case, except for in-store signage and marketing efforts, for most of the 20th century. Most retailers had store layouts and product sets designed to appeal to moms—without much thought to the kids who were with their moms during these shopping excursions. The classic example was mom picking out clothes, sending her son or daughter into the changing room, and then having them parade out for mom to say yeah or nay, or sending them back with a new selection that she had picked out.

Wow, times have changed! Retailers such as Target, Limited Too, and Wal-Mart, have recognized that mom and her kids are not just shopping together. In-fact, they are engaged in the shopping experience together. Stores and departments are set up to make it easy for kids and moms to find favorite products. Watch a mom and daughter enter a Limited Too store. Girls are delighted that the store is designed for them, and mom is delighted that her daughter is delighted.

Target, with its Dottie Loves brand, has made it easier for both girls and moms to find fun fashion accessories for tweens. On a recent store visit, I overheard a grandmother talking to her daughter (the mom) about her granddaughter. "She went straight for the camera. That was easy," she said as she put the Dottie Loves Camera into her cart. Target brought together an entire wall of fun fashion elements under the Dottie Loves branding, in clear, organized bins, shelves, and hangers. It was clear that the grandmother had asked the tween what she wanted for a gift, and everyone was pleased with how simple Target had made the shopping experience.

One of the most exciting initiatives targeting the Super Consumer is currently underway, not by a fashion or mass retailer, but by an electronics lifestyle retailer.

In late 2004 and early 2005, Best Buy told the marketplace (financial and business markets) that it was adopting a new business-changing approach to segmentation and defining new store approaches to better meet the needs of its customers. Its program, coined Customer Centricity, has moved from an original set of test stores to a phased rollout across the country. Customer Centricity, the Best Buy way, is about enhancing the shopping experience for its customers, from product selection, to store layout, to employee engagement.

Best Buy identified five priority customer segments one of which fits the definition of the Super Consumer. It acknowledges that it generally listened to 16-year-old boys and early adopters, but figured that moms really didn't factor into its customer equation. Nancy Brooks, the executive overseeing this initiative, in an *Advertising Age* article describes the situation they uncovered. "A lot of moms said they come to Best Buy because they're dragged by their husbands, or children, for approval. Not a lot of them enjoyed Best Buy as a shopping experience." So in essence, the 4i4l was coming into the store, but the experience was not optimal, to say the least.

Best Buy describes this segment as the "Jill" segment. According to a press release from the company this segment is "The busy suburban mom who wants to enrich her children's lives with technology and entertainment." Best Buy recognized a very important factor in this age of the Super Consumer. If you are only meeting the needs of one-half of this 4i4l consumer, the purchase opportunity may go somewhere else. On the other hand if you embrace the entire 4i4l, it will recognize and reward you for it.

So what are they doing? Some of the shopping-experience enhancements being tested for the Jill segment include personal shopping assistants, a "Just for Kids" area in the center of the store where toys and products can be demonstrated and played with, and products grouped together by feature, instead of brand. Best Buy's belief is that these and other enhancements will provide for a more enjoyable experience for mom and kid.

Travel and Leisure

Are Moms hearing kids with regard to a family vacation? Yes, according to both. As noted in Chapter 5, 46 percent of kids, aged 2 to 14, helped moms pick out the family vacation destination. With 34 million moms with kids in the U.S. we could easily assume that many hundreds of millions (or billions) of travel and leisure dollars are being directed to vacation destinations, hotels, resorts, and theme parks by the 4i4l.

And, not just the destination decision, but what to do when the family gets to the destination is completely up for discussion between the parents and their kids. The Fall 2003 *Simmons Kid Study* reported that 69 percent of kids say they mostly or sometimes get to choose things to do while on vacation. This means that once the trip has been set, parents want to be sure their kids are having a good time, and that means asking them what they want to do. Parents are asking, kids are talking, parents are listening, and the family activity decision is made—a classic 4i4l.

The nation's leading resort parks, Disney and Universal, have always known the power of the parent-child interaction. But historically they have addressed only the parents when advertising park vacations, relying on the trickle down effect to kids with an assumed nod of approval. Now more exciting rides are being added to their

parks to attract the interest of parents and older kids. And both Universal and Disney Resorts are more strongly expressing, visually in their messages, the excitement of their rides and activities for kids and parents. This is in contrast to previous focuses on branded property messages (i.e. Mickey and friends for Disney, Marvel Super-heroes and Nick characters for Universal).

Walt Disney World has taken its message about the excitement of its park to kids using a unique, viral-web-based MOG, or Massive Online Game, called Virtual Magic Kingdom. VMK as it is known, allows kids to experience many aspects of the park at the same time as other kids, in a game-based format, allowing a tremendous connection with the brand, and consequently, dialogue with their parents.

Virtual Magic Kingdom is touted in *Virtual World Reviews* as "the first virtual world that lets visitors supplement their online experience with a visit to a real world theme park." They also note that each Disney resort in Florida and California has a VMK Central area that lets players visit VMK to earn rare items. Characters created in person at a VMK Central area will be able to display a special "Born in Park" icon.

When the time comes to discuss vacations, these kids will already have a relationship going with The Walt Disney Resorts, and thus provide for easy dialogue within the 4i4l household.

Holiday Inn has made a bold move to appeal to both moms and kids with the introduction of Nickelodeon Family Suites by Holiday Inn. By partnering with Nickelodeon, Holiday Inn moves from a staid, old-fashioned image to one of incredible fun for kids and the whole family. Not just a hotel, it is now a destination of interest for both kids and parents. The hotel features rooms designed specifically to enhance the stay of families, with multi-room Kidsuites that provide for a private room for parents (big plus) and themed kids rooms with bunk beds—something for everyone.

We have seen a renewed interest by the travel category in the entire family unit as a result of increased awareness of the strength of kid-mom interactions and their effect on vacation spending decisions. From county travel bureaus, to zoos and museums, to national and international destinations, the ability to meet the travel and leisure needs of the 4i4l will have a direct effect on the opportunity to gain the family vacation dollar.

Automotive

What influence can kids have on the decision of parents with regards to transportation? For one thing, kids don't drive in most states until they are at least age 16. That said, they are merely passengers in the family car or van, being whisked by their parents to school, soccer games, the mall and let's not forget, vacation destinations. Or are they just passengers? Let's refer back to our *Influence Study* in Chapter 5, which shows that almost 40 percent of moms reported that their kid's input counted in their choice of an automobile. With approximately 52 million kids in the age range studied (2 to 14 year olds), 40 percent means that 21 million kids helped pick out family cars! Assuming that the average family has two kids means on the low end, 10.5 million households were involved in a 4i4l-type family automobile purchase. With the average price of a new car at about $20,000, this amounts to over $200 billion dollars! With $200 billion dollars at stake, it would make sense that car manufacturers would take note of the 4i4l, and make sure they are addressing their needs through product and message.

And that is exactly what a few smart car manufacturers have done. In research settings, kids can tell you what they like and what they don't like about cars, vans, and SUVs. Apparently they are telling their parents also, and the parents are listening. Go to any automobile showroom on a Saturday and you will see kids—lots of kids—with their parents. Most showrooms do little to accommodate kids, leaving them to play with the cars themselves, to the frowning faces of the sales staff. Realizing that kids are coming and will continue to come to the showroom with their parents, maybe it would make sense to make a gaming area with toy replicas of the brand's cars, video and/or computer games for older kids featuring auto software played from seats featuring cup holders, and other car accessories. How about a packet of information on family vans designed just for the kids, showing the features that are important to them? Just as Best Buy has done in the electronics retail category, there is so much potential to improve interaction with the 4i4l even in the automobile sales process.

Have any of the manufactures caught on—absolutely. Two great examples are Toyota and Chevrolet.

Toyota has recognized how important it is to mom that her kids are content with the family van. Toyota has aired a commercial that really brings this philosophy home. Some buttoned-up engineers announce that the design team has arrived; they open the door and in come a whole group of kids. Throughout the commercial there is a playful exchange of kids giving their two cents, and the Toyota engineers listening. From the number and placement of cup holders, to different sound and temperature zones, to trunk space (demonstrated by the ability to fit one girl's bicycle into the back), the kids make their needs known and Toyota provides the solution. What is most interesting about this commercial is that there is no mention of how well the car drives, how powerful an engine it has, or what type of suspension allows it to corner or brake so well. What it shows is how much your kids will like the van. Is that really important to today's mom? Yes, yes, and yes, and hats off to Toyota for recognizing it.

According to an August 1999 Chevrolet news release, in early 2000, Chevrolet made a bold leap forward in providing a travel solution that would optimally meet the need of the evolving Super Consumer. They teamed up with Warner Brothers, a venerable Goliath in family entertainment, to brand what they referred to as "the ultimate family road trip machine." The 2000 Chevrolet Venture line offered the first Warner Brothers Edition. It was a high-end priced, fully loaded minivan with unique cosmetic treatments, a fully integrated flip-down LCD video monitor for videos and gaming systems, and a console-mounted music system with remote control for the kids. The package also included "membership" benefits including free video/DVD discounts at Warner Brothers stores and Six Flags Theme parks and other amenities.

In 2005 Chevrolet migrated the Venture minivan with design changes and renamed the vehicle the "Uplander." Along with the introduction of the 2005 Uplander, Chevrolet announced another unique partnership, this time with Nickelodeon and PhatNoise. With this new partnership, Chevrolet was making a bold statement that it is committed to providing solutions for the 4i4l, including providing kids' favorite television programming and classic video games in their vehicles.

The entertainment system as shown on the Chevrolet Uplander web site.

The cutting-edge Mobile Digital Media Player, available in the Uplander, provides on-board content from Nickelodeon, Noggin and Nicktoons networks, as well as Capcom and other leading content and game providers. Craig Scruggs, Marketing Manager for the Chevy Uplander, said in an industry press release "We are excited to work with a leading-edge technology company and these top-tier entertainment companies to make access to the world of digital family entertainment in the car a reality." Chevrolet is working to create a unique experience in its Uplander minivan that provides for the entertainment environment kids have available at home. This new mobile environment also provides a driving experience that is more pleasurable for parents.

Homes, Interior Design and Home Décor

How about asking your 5-year-old to help make the family decision when the cost of the product is $200,000 or more. Seem outrageous? Not to many Super Consumer households. Deborah Snow Humiston, writing for the *Chicago Tribune* tells a great story:

> When Gisel and Nebo Rosairo were looking to build a new house, they settled on two models. Gisel liked one model, while Nebo liked the other. So they did what came naturally to them— they had their son, Nathan, cast the tie-breaking vote. Nathan sided with his father, so that was the model the Rosarios went with at Neumann Homes' Clublands development in Joliet.
>
> "He has a very outgoing personality. He fell in love with Cardiss (model)," Gisel Rosario said of their 5-year-old son. "There was nothing particular about the house, he just had a feeling and liked it. I wanted the other model because it had a loft."
>
> But Nathan's input didn't stop there. Nathan also took an active role in choosing some of the home's particulars, like carpeting in his bedroom, everything from the tile, to the toilet, to the counter in his bathroom, even the tile in the kitchen. "We feel he's unique and special. We feel it's important to include him. He'll always remember we included him in these decisions," Gisel Rosario said "We're a family and we should all be involved."

What Deborah Snow Humiston discovered about how parents are purchasing homes today is that it is not simply an adult-only decision as to what is best for the family. It is the 4i4l in action. I recently had the opportunity to talk with the father of two young daughters who is in the process of moving his family to a new city due to a business opportunity. He talked about the wonderful frankness of opinion offered by his girls when looking at new houses. "I like this." "Let's get the one with the pool," and my personal favorite, "This house stinks!" He said he could tell if the girls liked a house because they would immediately go upstairs to check out the bedrooms. If they don't like the house they get restless and bored. What is of most interest is that he was aware of his daughters' reactions and interest and welcomed them voicing their opinions.

Imagine the benefits to the new-home builder that incorporates the importance of meeting the needs of not only the parents, but also the children in the family. Offering up-front designs for playrooms and kid-friendly media centers could swing a decision in favor of one builder, other another builder who offers an unfinished or traditional basement or family room.

What happens after the 4i4l has decided on a new home purchase, or that it is time to update the current homestead? The rooms in the house probably need to be painted or wallpapered, filled with furniture, lights, and accessories. Designs and styles need to be determined down to the bathroom fixtures, the bedspreads, and the artwork. Again, we are now seeing manufactures and retailers catching on to the fact that their traditional consumer segment has changed.

The new millennium heralded many new and exciting things, and some of them included the first Pottery Barn Kids stores, and Pottery Barn Teen catalogs (now well over 100 pages each). Expanded sections of home products geared for kids and families appeared at retailers such as Target and others who now make it easier for moms and kids to find products designed to meet their desires and needs. Companies jumping on the band-wagon include historically stuffy furniture companies such as Ethan Allen, who has regrouped its kids lines as E.A. Kids with a goal of connecting with the kids, not just the parents who pay for the furniture. Mall kiosks do a brisk business selling huge bean-bag chairs during the holiday seasons. Parents are seldom buying these gigantic beanbag chairs for themselves, and at the prices that they command, the kids are seldom buying them with their own money. Mom and her kids are communicating and making the purchase decision together.

Gone are the days when the average family purchased furniture for their kids' rooms when they were 5, and kept it until they went to college, with furnishings as an afterthought based solely on functionality and decorations consisting of a few posters taped to the wall. Interior design changes in kids' bedrooms are taking place along the growing curve, in many instances spurred by kids' transition stages and welcomed by both moms and kids. For instance, moving from elementary to middle school, from junior high to high school, can immediately trigger mom and son or daughter to discuss a new look, a new style, and the need and desire for additional personal space and associated products (i.e. my own phone, my own television).

In a turning-point article on October 18, 2002, *The Wall Street Journal* took note of the spending power of tweens and teens regarding interior design products. Quoting an estimate on spending made by the authors of this book, Sarah Collins, the author of the article, said: "In all, the young-decorator set will spend about $17 billion this year on their rooms, double the amount less than a decade ago, according to The WonderGroup, a Cincinnati consulting company. They're getting tips from teen-apparel retailer Delia's, where housewares now account for 10 percent of catalog sales, up 50 percent from last year, and from Pier 1 Imports, which has started offering discounts to high-schoolers."

We generated this estimate of spending which amounts to about $386 per year per child aged 8 to 18 (kids living at home, not college dorms) based on what kids, their parents, and even their grandparents spend on an annualized basis on products that are now a mainstay in the sanctuary of a kid's bedroom: electronics (TVs, gaming systems, computers), furnishings, accessories, paint and wallpaper. Before long we were receiving calls from reporters all across America wanting to know more about this newly discovered marketplace, addressing it from both a consumer and business perspective. After all, what manufacturer or retailer wouldn't want to better address the needs of a consumer segment that spends $17 billion dollars in their category? What we could have told them is that the phenomenon isn't related to any single business category; the phenomenon is that there is a new consumer—**The Super Consumer.**

Bibliography

"Ad Inserts Drive the Women to the Store," Center for Media Research, May 20, 2004.

AOL/Digital Marketing Services, "When Moms Access the Internet," April 2002.

Bailey, Maria, *Marketing to Moms: Getting Your Share of the Trillion Dollar Market*, New York: Prima Publishing, 2002.

Bick, Julie, "Listen, Kid, You Have to be Tough to Make it in This Business Today," *The New York Times*, July 17, 2005.

Brazelton, T. Berry and Joshua D. Sparrow (2001), *Touchpoints Three to Six: Your Child's Emotional and Behavioral Development*, Cambridge, MA: Perseus Publishing, 2001.

Club Mom survey, (www.clubmom.com), Spring 2003.

Cole, M. and Cole, S., *The Development of Children*, New York: Worth Publishers, 2000.

Crain, William, *Theories of Development, Concepts and Applications*, 3rd Ed., Englewood Cliffs, NJ: Prentice Hall, 1992.

Cuneo, Alice Z., "Marketers Get Serious About the Third Screen," *Advertising Age*, July 11, 2005.

Current Population Reports, # 61 *Families by Size and Presence of Children, 1980-2003*,

U.S. Bureau of the Census, 2000.

"Disney, Warner, Sesame Calling Out To Ever-Younger Dialers" *Youth Markets Alert*, July 15, 2005.

Dobson, James, *The Strong-Willed Child: Birth through Adolescence*, Wheaton, IL: Tyndale House Publishing, Inc., 1978.

"Dreams Meet Reality," Roper Reports *Youth Report*, 2004.

"Effective Tactics for E-mail Marketing to Moms," Lucid Marketing

& Email Labs, June 2005.

Elias, Marilyn, "So Much Media, So Little Attention Span," *USA Today*, March 30, 2005.

"The Family-first Generation," *USA Today*, December 12, 2004.

Erickson, Martha Farrell, and Enola G. Aird, *The Motherhood Study: Fresh Insights on Mothers' Attitudes and Concerns*, New York: The Institute for American Values in conjunction with the University of Minnesota and the University of Connecticut, 2005.

Expenditures on Children by Families, U.S. Department of Agriculture, 2004.

"Exploring the Digital Generation: Implications for Education," White House Conference Center, September 23–24, 2003.

"Family Life is Becoming More Important to Many: Home Front," *Research Alert*, EPM Communications, January 21, 2005.

Fay, Jim and Charles Fay, *Love and Logic for Early Childhood: Practical Parenting from Birth to Six Years*. Golden, CO: The Love and Logic Press, 2000.

"Fertility of American Women," U.S. Bureau of the Census, 2000

Galinsky, Ellen, "Moms in Transition—Going Back to Work," Families and Work Institute, October 2004.

"Gen-X Women: Moving Up," *Business Week Online*, June, 14, 2002.

Greenspan, Robyn, "Moms Find Time Online," *ClickZ Stats Demographics*, May 7, 2004.

"Hot Jobs for the 21st Century," U.S. Bureau of Labor Statistics, May, 2003.

"Generation and Gender in the Workplace," New York: Families and Work Institute, 2005.

"Generation M: Media in the Lives of 8–18 Year Olds," (#7251), The Henry J. Kaiser Foundation, March 2005.

Harkness, Sara, Charles M. Super, Constance H. Keefer, Chemba S. Raghavan, and Elizabeth Kipp Campbell, "Ask the Doctor: The Negotiation of Cultural Models in American Parent-Pediatrician Discourse," *Parents' Cultural Belief Systems: Their Origins, Expressions, and Consequences*. New York: The Guilford Press, 1996.

"High Mileage Moms," Surface Transportation Policy Project, May 6, 1999.

Holt, John, *Escape from Childhood*, New York: E. P. Dutton & Co., Inc., 1974.

"Influence Grows but Wallets Shrink," *Youth Markets Alert*, New York: EPM Communications, December 1, 2003.

Jayson, Sharon, "Yep, Life'll Burst that Self-Esteem Bubble," *USA Today*, February 16, 2005.

Kayne, Kenneth, *Family Rules: Raising Responsible Children Without Yelling or Nagging*, New York: St. Martin's Press, 1984.

"Moms Give Best Advice, Say Kids," in *Marketing to Women*, New York: EPM Communications, December 2003.

"Moms Want Coupons, Discounts and Shipping in Email Offers," Center for Media Research, June 13, 2005.

Moore, Alan, "Peer Pleasure: Teen Connect," SMLXL website, March 2005.

Moore, Elizabeth et. al, "Passing the Torch: Intergenerational Influences as a Source of Brand Equity," *Journal of Marketing*, Vol. 66, April 2002.

"Most Mothers Say Advertisers Don't Recognize Their Needs as Mothers," Center for Media Research, www.mediapost.com, November 3, 2004.

"Motivated by Their Constituency: Family Dynamics are Key to the Mom's Market," in *Marketing to Women*, New York: EPM Communications, 2001.

"National Study of the Changing Workforce—Highlights," New York: Work and Families Institute, 2002.

Neeley, Sabrina, and Tim Coffey, "Who's Your Momma?" *Advertising & Marketing to Children*, July-Sept 2004.

Pastore, Michael, "Moms Using Web to Bring Families Together," ClickZ Stats Demographics, March 5, 2001.

Paul, Pamela, "Getting Inside Gen-Y," *American Demographics,* September 2001.

Pogue, David, "In One Stroke, Podcasting Hits Mainstream," *The New York Times,* July 28, 2005.

"Product Placement Gets Brands in Front of Highly Active Teen Segment," *Youth Markets Alert*, April 15, 2005.

Rust, Langbourne, Dr., "Please, Please, Please: Understanding Purchase Influence," Speech at SRI Marketing to Kids conference, September 22, 1994.

Rust, Langbourne, Dr., "Parents and Children Shopping Together: A New Approach to the Qualitative Analysis of Observational Data," *Journal of Advertising Research*, Vol. 33, No. 4,1993.

Saunders, Christopher, "Moms, Hispanics Increasing Web Use," *ClickZ News*, May 7, 2002.

Sears, William and Martha Sears, *The Attachment Parenting Book: A Commonsense Guide to Understanding and Nurturing Your Baby*, New York: Little, Brown and Company, 2001.

Siegel, David, et. al., *The Great Tween Buying Machine*, Ithaca, NY: Paramount Market Publishing, 2002.

Silver Stork Panel Survey, October 2003.

Simmons Market Research, Kid Simmons, Fall, 2004.

Simmons Market Research, Full-year data, Fall, 2004.

Spock, Benjamin, *Dr. Spock's The School Years: The Emotional and Social Development of Children*, Martin T. Stein, Ed., New York: Pocket Books, 2001.

"Students in NetDay Community Projects, Speak Out on Internet Use," Press Release, February 28, 2003.

"Study: Brain Grows Furiously," *The New York Times*, March 9, 2000.

"Technology in Schools: A Means, Not an End," Harris Interactive *DistrictWise*, May 2005.

"The Consensual Kid," Roper Reports *Youth Report,* 2004.

"The Influence of Millennials," *Exploring the Digital Generation*, Yankelovich *Youth Monitor*, September 23, 2003.

The State of Our Nation's Youth, 2003-2004, Alexandria, VA: Horatio Alger Foundation, 2004.

"Time & Money: Teen/Tween Spending Trends," New York: EPM Communications, April 2004.

"Toys Top Kids' Purchases, But Boys Are More Likely Than Girls to Buy Them," *Youth Markets Alert*, New York: EPM Communications, November 1, 2002.

Tripp, Tedd, *Shepherding a Child's Heart*, Wapwallopen, PA: Shepherd Press, 1995.

Walling, Claudia, "A Case for Staying Home," *Time* Magazine, March 15, 2004.

Watson, John B., *Behaviorism*, New York: W.W. Norton & Company, 1924.

Wegert, Tessa, "Tapping the Mom Market," www.clickz.com, November 2004.

Williams, Alex, "Nag Factor Has Parents of Teens in a Material Spin," *The New York Times* news service, May 30, 2005.

"Zero to Six: Electronic Media in the Lives of Infants, Toddlers, and Preschoolers," (#3378), The Henry J. Kaiser Family Foundation, October 2003.

Index

Meet the Authors

David L. Siegel

Dave has been marketing to kids and their moms for more than 25 years. After several years of classic consumer packaged goods marketing for such companies as Procter & Gamble, Bristol Myers Drackett, and others, Dave moved over to the advertising and consulting field where he became enamored with the kids marketplace.

As one of the first classic consumer marketers to realize the potential of marketing to kids, Dave has had the opportunity of helping dozens of companies in just about every industry realize and capitalize on the potential of marketing to kids and their moms. Among his many clients have been such companies as Hasbro, Warner-Lambert, Motorola, JVC, Borden, Chiquita, Curad, Chupa Chups, Evenflo, Disney, Lipton, ConAgra, and Procter & Gamble.

Over the years, Dave has addressed such groups as the U.S. Olympic Committee, Grocery Manufacturer's Association, Color Marketing Group, School Home & Office Association as well as several AMA chapters and the Retail Merchandising Conference regarding kids marketing. He has chaired or spoken at virtually every kids marketing conference in the country as well as Europe and Asia, and is also on the advisory board for KidPower and Marketing and Advertising to Kids.

In 1998, Dave joined forces with Tim Coffey and Greg Livingston and became president of WonderGroup, specializing in marketing and advertising to kids and their moms in the United States.

Dave, his wife Jan, and their children Robin, Adam, Lauren, and Tiffany live in Cincinnati.

Timothy J. Coffey

Tim is the CEO and Chairman of Wondergroup, and its new product development agency, LaunchForce. He has helped such companies as Kellogg's, Kodak, Reebok, Heinz, Johnson & Johnson, ConAgra and others to develop successful marketing programs that appeal to kids, tweens, teens, and their moms.

Consumer behavior has been Tim's professional passion for more than 20 years. Early in his career, he worked as a market researcher for Procter & Gamble, where he uncovered consumer insights and preferences in the laundry, household cleaning products, and beauty care categories.

His views on marketing to moms and kids began to develop while he was in brand management for Procter & Gamble, working on such brands as Hawaiian Punch and Sunny D. Tim also worked as marketing director for Tupperware, where he helped reinvent the brand's image and product line to appeal to today's new moms.

His most profound experience, however, is gained on a daily basis from his own family. Together with his wife, Jill, Tim has a living "focus group" of four girls—Sara 19, Kathleen 16, Shannon 14, and Elizabeth 9.

Gregory Livingston

Greg got his first taste of youth and family advertising early in his career at New York advertising agencies, including assignments on the Nestlé and Sitmar Cruise accounts. Following a range of agency roles, Greg jumped to the client side spending 10 years as vice president of marketing and advertising for LCA-Vision. LCA-Vision, a medical services organization, evolved into the nation's largest network of laser centers for correction of myopia (a procedure now called LASIK).

After LCA-Vision went public in 1996, Greg got the itch to get back into the agency business and joined Sive/Young & Rubicam, where he had the fortunate opportunity to be only two offices away from Dave Siegel. Greg immediately became enamored with the realm of youth marketing as Dave espoused the principles and fascinating nuances of how to communicate to the younger generation.

Leaving with Dave in 1998 to join Tim Coffey in the formation of WonderGroup, Greg has been involved in youth and mom–focused product development and advertising for companies including Hasbro, Airheads Candies, Chiquita, Kellogg's, Reebok, ConAgra, Pillsbury, Heinz, Johnson & Johnson, and Procter & Gamble. Greg, along with Tim and Dave, has chaired and/or presented topical subjects at youth conferences and corporations across the country.

Greg and his wife Paula, a clinical social worker who specializes in adolescents, have three boys, Ryan 13 and Graham 11, and Ian 4.